THE COMPLETE WORKS OF WILLIAM SHAKESPEARE [abridged]

THE COMPLETE WORKS OF WILLIAM SHAKESPEARE
  [ABRIDGED]
By Adam Long, Daniel Singer, and Jess Winfield
©1987 by Adam Long, Daniel Singer, and Jess Winfield
"Rap Othello" ©1989 by Adam Long and Jess Winfield

ISBN 1-55783-271-4

APPLAUSE BOOKS
211 West 71st Street
New York, NY 10023
Phone (212) 496-7511
Fax: (212) 721-2856

THE COMPLETE WORKS OF WILLIAM SHAKESPEARE [abridged]

By Adam Long, Daniel Singer, and Jess Winfield

APPLAUSE
NEW YORK • LONDON

The Complete Works of William Shakespeare [abridged] was first performed [more or less in its entirety] by the authors on June 19, 1987, at the Paramount Ranch in Agoura, California, and subsequently at the 1987 Edinburgh Festival Fringe. Additional premieres with different casts include the Arts Theatre, London [1992], the Westside Theater Off-Broadway [1995], and the Criterion Theatre in London's West End [1996].

THE ORIGINAL CAST:
Adam Long
Daniel Singer
Jess Winfield

THE ORIGINAL LONDON CAST:
ADAM LONG
REED MARTIN
JESS WINFIELD

THE NEW YORK CAST:
Christopher Duva
Peter Jacobson
Jon Patrick Walker

NOTE: The script is written for three actors. In performance, the actors should substitute their own names for "Adam," "Jess," and "Daniel." Where Shakespearean characters appear in the script, the character name is preceded by the actor's initial: i.e., A/JULIET means Adam is playing Juliet, D/ROMEO means Daniel is playing Romeo, J/HAMLET means Jess is playing Hamlet, etc. More or less "Shakespearean" dialogue appears in double quotation marks [" "].

ALSO NOTE: Because the show comments on contemporary events to place Shakespeare's works in modern context, it's absolutely essential to keep the show fresh and timely by updating the many topical references as events warrant. We sincerely hope, for example, that by the time you read this, you won't have Newt Gingrich to kick around anymore. Please, have some fun and come up with your very own put-downs of annoying famous people where required.

ALSO ALSO NOTE: Far be it from us writers to tell you directors and actors how to stage the show; but having performed it ourselves about a billion times, we'd thought we'd offer you a smidgen of performance advice. The show was developed through improvisation, and is predicated on the conceit that these three guys are making the whole thing up as they go along, getting by on blind enthusiasm and boundless energy wherever they lack talent or any real clue about Shakespeare's work. It's important that the actors be genuinely surprised by each line, each action, and each turn of events. For example, although the audience participation section of Act Two is presented here based on our broad experience with how audiences generally respond, each audience is different. The actors should respond honestly to the audience's performance, and their own, rather than stick blindly to the written text. The whole show should feel so spontaneous that the audience will never really know if that screaming audience member was a plant [*She wasn't.*], if Daniel really stepped on Adam's crotch in Romeo and Juliet [*He didn't.*], or if Jess really watches General Hospital every day [*Usually just Tuesdays and Thursdays.*].

Above all, have fun.

And do it FASTER!

ACT ONE

The pre-show music, the end of the 'Jupiter' section of Gustav Holz' 'The Planets,' reaches its crashing climax. Lights come up on the stage. The set consists of a low-budget representation of an Elizabethan theater in the fashion of Shakespeare's Globe, with four escapes, upstage right and left, downstage right and left, and an additional entrance up center. Stage right there is a 'Masterpiece Theater' style narrator's set, which prominently features a book: The Complete Works of William Shakespeare. *After a beat,* DANIEL *enters from down left, ostensibly a house manager.*

DANIEL: Good evening, ladies and gentlemen, and welcome to the _____ Theater and tonight's performance of the *Complete Works of William Shakespeare [abridged]*. I have a few brief announcements before we get under way. The use of flash photography and the recording of this show by any means, audio or video, is strictly prohibited by the management. Also, please refrain from eating, drinking, or smoking—anything—during the performance. For your convenience, toilets are located in the lobby. Also, please take a moment now to locate the exit nearest your seat. [*Points to exits, in the manner of an airline flight attendant.*] Should the theater experience a sudden loss of pressure, oxygen masks [*Pulls one from his jacket pocket.*] will drop automatically. Simply place the mask over your nose and mouth, and continue to breathe normally. If you are at the theater with a small child, please place your own mask on first, and let the little bugger fend for himself. Allow me to introduce myself. My name is Daniel Singer, and tonight, my two partners and I are going to attempt a feat which we believe to be unprecedented in the history of theater. [*He goes to the narrator's set and hefts the*

Complete Works *tome.*] That is, to capture, in a single theatrical experience, the magic, the genius, the towering grandeur of *The Complete Works of William Shakespeare.* [*Glances at the huge book in his hand.*] Now we have a lot to get through tonight, so at this time I'd like to introduce a gentleman who is one of America's preeminent Shakespearean scholars. He has a bachelor's degree from the University of California at Berkeley, where I believe he read two books about William Shakespeare. He is here tonight to provide a brief preface to *The Complete Works of William Shakespeare [abridged].* Please welcome me in joining Mr. Jess Winfield.

[JESS *enters in a tweedy suit and spectacles. He shakes hands with* DANIEL, *who hands him the book then retires to the armchair to listen.*]

JESS: Thank you, Daniel, and good evening, ladies and gentlemen. [*Clinging to the* Complete Works *book adoringly, he begins professorially, as if lecturing a class of students.*] William Shakespeare: playwright, poet, actor, philosopher; a man whose creative and literary genius have had an immeasurably profound influence upon the consciousness and culture of the entire English-speaking world. And yet, how much do we inhabitants of the twentieth century know and appreciate the tremendous body of work contained in this single volume? Too little, I would argue. I believe I could illustrate this point by conducting a brief poll here, among our audience. [*To the light booth.*] If I may have the house lights for just a moment, please?

[*The house lights come up.*]

Now, you are a theater-going crowd, no doubt of above-average cultural and literary awareness, and yet if I may just have a brief show of hands, how many of you have ever seen or read any play by William Shakespeare? Any contact at all with the Bard, just raise your hands...

[*Almost everyone raises a hand.* JESS *shrinks away to confer, sotto voce, with* DANIEL.]

JESS: I think they might know more than we do, maybe we better get outta here.

DANIEL: Don't worry about it.

JESS: No, we should really start running NOW.

DANIEL: They don't know Shakespeare from shinola, just keep going.

JESS: What should I do?

DANIEL: [*Mouthing.*] Narrow it down.

JESS: What?

DANIEL: [*Whispering.*] Narrow it down.

JESS: [*To audience.*] Let's see if we can narrow it down a bit, shall we? How many of you have ever seen or read, let's say, *All's Well That Ends Well*?

[*Perhaps a third of the audience raises their hands.*]

JESS: Yes, that seems to be separating the wheat from the chaff rather nicely. Let's see if we can find out who the true Shakespeare trivia champs are tonight. Has anybody ever seen or read *King John*? *King John*, anyone?

[ADAM, *sitting on an aisle seat in the third row and wearing street garb, raises his hand.* JESS *spots him.*]

JESS: You have, really? Would you mind telling us what it's about?

ADAM: It's about a hunchback.

[JESS *glowers for a moment, then pointing an accusing finger at* ADAM.]

JESS: This is exactly what I'm talking about. Oh, right, you laugh, ladies and gentlemen, you scoff, but let he among you who is free from sin live in a glass house! For that face, ladies and gentlemen, that face represents all your faces. [JESS *leaves the stage and begins to bear down on* ADAM.] That empty brain represents your empty brains. Those glazed eyes are your glazed eyes, these teeth

[*Grabbing* ADAM'S *face and showing it to the audience.*]

JESS: [*Cont'd.*] are your teeth, and they cry out, 'FLOSS ME!' [*As he returns to the stage.*] Ladies and gentlemen, I submit to you that our society's collective capacity to comprehend—much less attain—the genius of a William Shakespeare has been systematically shrunken by sitcoms, sodomized by soap operas and reamed by Rush Limbaugh. But have no fear! Your intellectual salvation is here!

DANIEL: Sing it, brother!

JESS: [*He is beginning to metamorphose into a fire-and-brimstone evangelist.*] We descend among you on a mission from God and the literary muse, to spread the holy word of the Bard to the masses.

DANIEL: Testify!

JESS: To help you take those first halting steps OUT of the twentieth century quagmire of Donahue, Geraldo and Oprah Jessy Raphael, and into the future!

DANIEL: Amen!

JESS: A glorious future! A future where manly men wear pink tights with pride! A future where this book [*Indicating the* Complete Works.] will be found in every hotel room in the world! This is my dream, ladies and gentlemen, and it begins here, tonight. Join us in taking those first steps down the path toward the brave new world of intellectual redemption by opening your hearts.

[DANIEL *picks up a collection plate and begins to walk through the audience, soliciting donations.*]

JESS: Yes, please open your hearts—and your pocketbooks. Or simply charge your donations to your MasterCard or Visa by phoning 976-BARD right now! Give us your cash, if we be friends, and deduct it when the tax year ends! On with the show, and may the Bard be with you! Thank you, and Hallelujah!!

[*The house lights fade as* DANIEL *returns to the stage, shakes* JESS'S *hand and exchanges the collection plate for the* Complete Works *book.* JESS *finds a large bill in the plate and tucks it in his pocket as he exits.*]

DANIEL: Those of you who own a copy of this book know that no collection is complete without a brief biography of the life of William Shakespeare. Providing this portion of the show will be the third member of the troupe; please welcome to the stage Mr. Adam Long.

[ADAM *comes to the stage. As he reaches to shake* DANIEL'S *hand, he drops a small stack of 3x5 index cards: his notes. He hastily picks them up.*]

DANIEL: Oops, sorry. Let me help you . . .

ADAM: No, don't touch them. They go in an order.

DANIEL: Okay, okay. [*Sits in chair.*]

ADAM: [*Trying to quickly put his notes back in order.*] Hi. As you can see, I'm not an audience member, I completely fooled you. I've just been taking a few notes on Shakespeare's life so we could get the show off to a good start, so you could know all the stuff he did an' everything . . .

DANIEL: [*Sotto voce.*] Just get on with it.

ADAM: Okay, okay. [*He begins reading from the index cards.*] William Shakespeare. William Shakespeare was born in 1564 in the town of Stratford-upon-Avon, Warwickshire. The third of eight children, he was the eldest son of John Shakespeare, a locally prominent merchant, and Mary Arden, daughter of a Roman. [*He pauses, flips to the next card. With no comprehension of what he's reading.*] Catholic member of the landed gentry. In 1582 he married Anne Hathaway, a farmer's daughter... [*To* DANIEL.] Heh. Farmer's daught— [*But* DANIEL *cuts him off with a stern look.*]

ADAM: [*Reading again.*] He is supposed to have left Stratford after he was caught poaching in the deer park of a local justice of the peace. [*Next card.*] Shakespeare arrived in London in 1588. By 1592, he had achieved success as an actor and a playwright. After 1608 his dramatic production lessened, and it seems that he spent more time in Stratford. [*Next card.*] There he dictated to his secretary, Rudolf Hess, the work *Mein Kampf*, in which he set forth his program for the restoration of Germany to a dominant position in Europe. After reoccupying the Rhineland zone between France and Germany, and annexing Austria, the Sudetenland, and the remainder of Czechoslovakia [*Next card.*], Shakespeare invaded Poland on September 1, 1939, thus precipitating World War II. [*To* DANIEL.] I never knew that before.

[DANIEL *gestures to him to wrap it up.*]

ADAM: [*Reads rapidly.*] Shakespeare remained in Berlin when the Russians entered the city, and committed suicide with his mistress, Eva Braun. [*Next card.*] He lies buried in the church at Stratford. Thank you.

[ADAM *bows.* DANIEL *rises, shakes his hand, and hurries him offstage.*]

DANIEL: Now, without further ado, we are proud to prevent *The Complete Works of William Shakespeare [abridged]!*

[*Blackout. A pretentious heavy-metal version of 'Greensleeves' crashes through the sound system. The music ends with an enormous cymbal crash. A light comes up to reveal* JESS *in Shakespearean attire and Converse high-top canvas sneakers, sitting in the Masterpiece Theater chair and holding the* Complete Works *book. He regards the audience smugly for a moment, opens the book, and reads.*]

JESS: "All the world's a stage,
And all the men and women merely players.
They have their exits and their entrances
And one man in his time plays many parts."

One man in his time plays many parts. How true. Ladies and gentlemen, where better to begin our exploration of the complete works of the greatest of all English playwrights than in Verona, Italy—with one of his most beloved plays: *Romeo and Juliet.*

[ADAM *and* DANIEL *enter, also in Elizabethan costume and Converse high-tops, and begin warm-ups and stretches.*]

JESS: Of course it would be impossible to portray all the roles in *Romeo and Juliet* with just three actors. That's why we're using TWO. That's right, Adam and Daniel will be attempting to portray all of the major character roles in *Romeo and Juliet*, while I fill in with bits of narration. After extensive textual research and analysis, we have decided to begin our abbreviated version of *Romeo and Juliet* with ... the Prologue.

ADAM AND DANIEL: [*Simultaneously, with synchronized gestures.*] "Two households, both alike in dignity,
In fair Verona where we lay our scene,
From ancient grudge break to new mutiny

Where civil blood makes civil hands unclean.
From forth the fatal loins of these two foes
A pair of star-crossed lovers take their life,
Whose misadventured, piteous o'erthrows
Do, with their death, bury their parents' strife."

[*They bow.* DANIEL *lifts* ADAM *into a balletic exit, then follows him off.*]

JESS: Act One, Scene One:
In the street meet two men tall and handsome:
One, Benvolio;

[ADAM *enters as* BENVOLIO.]

The other named Sampson.

[DANIEL *enters as* SAMPSON.]

Their hatred fueled by an ancient feud
For one serves Capulet, the other Montague . . . d.

A/BEN: [*Singing.*] O, I like to rise when the sun she rises, early in the morning . . .

D/SAM: [*Singing simultaneously.*] I had a little doggie and his name was Mr. Jiggs; I sent him to the grocery store to fetch a pound of figs . . .

[*They see each other. Simultaneously.*]

A/BEN: [*Aside.*] Ooo, it's him. I hate his guts. I swear to God I'm gonna kill him.

D/SAM: [*Aside.*] Ooo, it's him. I hate his family, hate his dog, hate 'em all.

[*They smile and bow to each other. As they cross to opposite sides of the stage,* SAMPSON *bites his thumb at* BENVOLIO, *who trips* SAMPSON *in return.*]

A/BEN: Do you bite your thumb at me, sir?

D/SAM: No sir, I do but bite my thumb.

A/BEN: Do you bite your thumb at me, sir?

D/SAM: No sir, I do not bite my thumb at you, sir, but I do bite my thumb. Do you quarrel, sir?

A/BEN: Quarrel, sir? No, sir.

D/SAM: But if you do, sir, I am for you. I serve as good a man as you.

A/BEN: No better.

D/SAM: Yes. Better.

A/BEN: You lie!

[*They fly at each other. Massive fight scene.* BENVOLIO *chases* SAMPSON *offstage.* BENVOLIO *flings a stunt-dummy* SAMP-SON *onstage, stomps on it, twists its legs, bites its toe.* DANIEL *enters as the* PRINCE.]

D/PRINCE: Rebellious subjects, enemies to the peace.

A/BEN: Uh-oh, it's the Prince.

D/PRINCE: [*Perturbed.*] Ahem!

A/BEN: Sorry, the character formerly known as Prince.

D/PRINCE: "Profaners of this neighbor-stained steel.
You, Capulet, shall go along with me.
Benvolio, come you this afternoon
To know our farther pleasure in this case.

[D/PRINCE *exits with dummy.*]

A/BEN: O where is Romeo? Saw you him today?
Right glad I am he was not at this fray.
But see, he comes!

[DANIEL *makes a grand entrance as* ROMEO, *wearing a very silly wig and wistfully sniffing at a plastic rose.*]

Romeo, he cried.
I'll know his grievance or be much denied.

[*They dance a conversational pas de deus during the following lines.*]

Good morrow, coz.

D/ROMEO: Is the day so young?

A/BEN: But new struck nine.

D/ROMEO: Ay, me. Sad hours seem long.

A/BEN: What sadness lengthens Romeo's hours?

D/ROMEO: Not having that which, having, makes them short.

A/BEN: In love?

D/ROMEO: Out.

A/BEN: Out of love?

D/ROMEO: Out of her favor where I am in love.

A/BEN: Alas that love, so gentle in his view,
Should be so rough and tyrannous in proof.

D/ROMEO: Alas that love, whose view is muffl'd still,
Should without eyes see pathways to his will.

BOTH: [*As the dance concludes with a sudden wistful tableau.*] O!

A/BEN: Go ye to the feast of Capulets.
There sups the fair Rosaline whom thou so lovest
With all the admired beauties of Verona.
Go thither and compare her face with some that I shall
show
And I shall make thee think thy swan a crow. [*Exits.*]

D/ROMEO: I'll go along, no such sight to be shown,
But to rejoice in splendor of my own." [*Exits.*]

JESS: So much for Act One.

Now to the feast of Capulet
Where Romeo is doomed to meet his Juliet.
And where, in a scene of timeless romance,
He'll try to get into Juliet's pants.

[ADAM *enters as* JULIET, *wearing a wig even sillier than* ROMEO'S. *She dances.* ROMEO *enters, sees her, and is immediately smitten.*]

D/ROMEO: "O, she doth teach the torches to burn bright.
Did my heart love 'til now? Forswear it, sight.
For I ne'er saw true beauty 'til this night.

[*Takes* JULIET's *hand.*]

If I profane with my unworthiest hand
This holy shrine, the gentle fine is this:
My lips, two blushing pilgrims ready stand
To smooth that rough touch with a tender kiss.

[JULIET *has nearly reached a climax during* ROMEO'S *speech . . . but the instant* ROMEO'S *lips touch her hand, she recoils.*]

A/JULIET: Good pilgrim, you do wrong your hands too much,
Which mannerly devotion shows in this;
For saints have hands that pilgrims' hands do touch
And palm to palm is holy palmers' kiss.

D/ROMEO: Have not saints lips, and holy palmers too?

A/JULIET: Ay, pilgrim. Lips that they must use in prayer.

D/ROMEO: O then, dear saint, let lips do what hands do.

[ADAM *has no wish to be kissed and struggles with* DANIEL *over the following lines.*]

A/JULIET: Saints do not move, though grant for prayers' sake.

D/ROMEO: Then move not, while my prayers' effect I take.

A/JULIET: Then from my lips the sin that they have took.

D/ROMEO: Sin from my lips? O trespass sweetly urged. Give me my sin again."

ADAM: [*Breaking character.*] I don't wanna kiss you, man.

DANIEL: It's in the script.

[ADAM *knees* DANIEL *in the groin. He crumples to the floor in pain.*]

A/JULIET: "You kiss by the book." [*Puts a hand to his ear, as if hearing an offstage call.*] Oh, coming, mother!

[ADAM *looks around, curses under his breath. He runs into the audience house left, and clambers awkwardly up a support pillar. If no pillar is available, he may use* JESS'S *shoulders, or a tree, or anything else suitably awkward; but under no circumstances use an actual balcony!.*]

D/ROMEO: "Is she a Capulet? Ay, so I fear. The more is my unrest."

[*Breaking character, to* ADAM.] What are you doing?

A/JULIET: The Balcony Scene.

D/ROMEO: "But soft, what light through yonder window breaks?

A/JULIET: O Romeo, Romeo, wherefore art thou Romeo? [*His dress is immodestly wide open as he clings to the pillar.*] Deny thy father and refuse thy name..."

[*He spots a member of the audience directly underneath him.*] I know what you're lookin' at, buddy! [*He closes his legs indignantly. They are now wrapped tightly around the pole.*]

Or if thou wilt not, be but sworn my love,
And I'll no longer be a Capulet.
What's in a name, anyway? That which we call a nose
By any other name would still smell.
O Romeo..."

O Romeo! Romeo! [*Referring to the pole.*] Who needs Romeo!?!

"... doff thy name, which is no part of thee,
Take all myself. [*Plummets to the floor.*]

D/ROMEO: I take thee at thy word. Call me but love,
And I shall be new-baptiz'd. Henceforth
I shall never be Romeo."

A/JULIET: What did you just say?

D/ROMEO: ... Call me but love,
And I'll be new baptized. Henceforth—

A/JULIET: Call you butt-love?!

D/ROMEO: Henceforth, I never shall be Romeo.

A/JULIET: You're butt-love!

D/ROMEO: I never shall be Romeo.

A/JULIET: Butt-love, butt-love, butt-love—

[DANIEL *snatches* ADAM'S *hand, and* ADAM *snaps out of it.*]

"What man art thou? Art thou not Romeo,
And a Montague?

D/ROMEO: Neither, fair maid, if either thee dislike.

A/JULIET: Dost thou love me then? I know thou wilt say aye,
And I will take thy word. Yet if thou swearest,
Thou mayest prove false. O Romeo, if thou dost love,
Pronounce it faithfully.

D/ROMEO: Lady, by yonder blessed moon, I swear—

A/JULIET: O swear not by the moon!

D/ROMEO: What shall I swear by?"

[JULIET *points to a woman in the audience.*]

D/ROMEO: Lady, by yonder blessed virgin, I swear—

A/JULIET: [*Referring to the woman.*] I don't think so. "No,
Do not swear at all. Although I joy in thee,
I have no joy in this contract tonight.
It is too rash, too sudden, too unadvised,
Too like the lightning, which doth cease to be
Ere one can say it lightens. Sweet, good night.

[JULIET *is ready to say* "good night" *at the upstage door, but* ROMEO *is on another planet, caught up in a series of gestures.*]

A/JULIET: Sweet, good night...yo, butt-love, over here.

[ROMEO *snaps out of it and joins her upstage.*]

D/ROMEO: [*On one knee.*] O wilt thou leave me so unsatisfied?

A/JULIET: What satisfaction canst thou have?

D/ROMEO: The exchange of thy love's faithful vows for mine.

A/JULIET: I gave thee mine before thou didst request it."

[JULIET *sits on* ROMEO'S *knee, and* ROMEO *nuzzles into her breast.*]

A/JULIET: Whoa, whoa...second base is for second date, sweetie.

"Three words, gentle Romeo, and then good night indeed.
If that thy bent of love be honorable,
Thy purpose marriage, send word tomorrow.

[*She rises and crosses downstage center to address the audience with great emotion.*]

Good night, good night; parting is such sweet sorrow—"

Really, it is. [*She exits, blowing a kiss to the love-struck* ROMEO.] Bye, butt-love!

D/ROMEO: "Sleep dwell upon thine eyes, peace in thy breast.
O that I were sleep and peace, so sweet to rest." [*Freezes.*]

JESS: Lo, Romeo did swoon with love;

By Cupid he'd been crippl't;
But Juliet had a loathsome coz
Whose loathsome name was Tybalt.

[ADAM *enters as* TYBALT, *snarling, carrying two foils.*]

A/TYBALT: "Romeo, the love I bear thee can afford
No better term than this: thou art a villain.
Therefore turn and draw.

D/ROMEO: Tybalt, I do protest, I never injured thee,
But love thee, better than thou canst devise.

A/TYBALT: Thou wretched boy, I am for you!

[TYBALT *throws* ROMEO *a foil.* ROMEO *closes his eyes and extends the blade, neatly impaling the advancing* TYBALT. *The whole "swordfight" has taken less than a second.*]

A/TYBALT: O I am slain." [ADAM *bows and exits.*]

[JESS *flips frantically through pages of the book.* DANIEL *rushes over to him, confused by* TYBALT'S *o'er-hasty exit.*]

DANIEL: Now what do we do?

JESS: I don't know. He skipped all this stuff. [*Points to a place in the book.*] Go to here.

DANIEL: Okay. [*Exits.*]

JESS: Moving right along...
From Tybalt's death onwards, the lovers are cursed,
Despite the best efforts of Friar and Nurse;
Their fate pursues them, they can't seem to duck it...
And at the end of Act Five, they both kick the bucket.

[JULIET *enters, riding an imaginary horse, humming the 'William Tell Overture.'*]

A/JULIET: "Gallop apace, you fiery-footed steeds,
And bring in cloudy night immediately.

Come civil night! Come night! Come Romeo,
Thou day in night! Come, gentle night!
Come loving, black-brow'd night!
O night night night night...
Come come come come come!"
[*Aside to audience.*] I didn't write it.
"And bring me my Romeo!

[DANIEL *enters as the* NURSE, *wailing. He is amply padded with large falsies... at least one of which is dangling outside his dress. After* ADAM *points this out, and the errant breast is replaced, the scene continues.*]

A/JULIET: O it is my nurse. Now nurse, what news?

D/NURSE: Alack the day, he's gone, he's killed, he's dead!

A/JULIET: Can heaven be so envious?

D/NURSE: Romeo, Romeo! Who ever would have thought it? Romeo!

A/JULIET: What devil art thou to torment me thus? This torture should be roared in dismal hell. Hath Romeo slain himself?"

[*They both go into a blind panic, running around and shrieking hysterically.*]

A/JULIET: [*Accosting a man in the audience.*] O no! He's dead! He's gone, he's killed, he's dead, what are you doing tonight?

D/NURSE: "I saw the wound, I saw it with mine own eyes— God save the mark—here in his manly breast."

A/JULIET: Is Romeo slaughter'd and is Tybalt dead?
My dearest cousin and my dearer lord?
Then dreadful trumpets sound the general doom!

D/NURSE: No, Juliet, no! No!
Tybalt is gone and Romeo banished.
Romeo that kill'd Tybalt, he is banished!

A/JULIET: [*After a tremendous double-take.*] O Go
hand shed Tybalt's blood?

D/NURSE: It did, it did, alas the day it did."

[*They sob and scream hysterically, finally pick up mugs and throw water in each other's faces.*]

A/JULIET AND D/ROMEO: [*Bowing.*] Thank you.

[NURSE *exits, leaving* JULIET *alone to assess the situation.*]

A/JULIET: Now Romeo lives, whom Tybalt would have slain.
Well, that's good, isn't it?

[*Probably no response from the audience.*]

A/JULIET: I said, isn't that good?

[*Audience murmurs, "Yeah!"*]

A/JULIET: Damn straight.
And Tybalt is dead, who would have killed my husband.
Well, that's good, isn't it?

[*Audience responds.*]

A/JULIET: So why do I feel like shit?
It's not a good day for Juliet, it's an icky poo-poo ca-
ca wee-wee pee-pee weebles-wobble-but-they-don't-fall-
down-day...

[DANIEL *enters as* FRIAR LAURENCE. *He is an actual Italian.*]

A/JULIET: O, Friar Laurence! Romeo is banished an' Tybalt is
slain an' I've got cramps an' that not-so-fresh feeling—

D/FRIAR: "Juliet, I already know thy grief. Take-a thou this
vial-a, and this distilled liquor drink-a thou off-a. And
presently through alla thy veins-a shall run a cold anna
drowsy-a humor-a."

A/JULIET: [*Takes bottle and drinks.*] O, I feel a cold and-a drowsy-
a humor-a running through my veins.

/FRIAR: Told-a you so.

[FRIAR LAURENCE *exits. The poison goes to* JULIET'S *head immediately.*]

A/JULIET: Hey, this feels kinda nice! Uh-oh. I'm George Bush in Japan ...

[JULIET *begins to convulse, vomits on several people in the front row, and finally dies a dramatic death.* ROMEO *enters. He sees* JULIET *and rushes to her prone body, accidentally stepping on her crotch while doing so.*]

D/ROMEO: "O no! My love, my wife!
Death, that hath suck'd the honey of thy breath,
Hath no power yet upon thy beauty.
O Juliet, why art thou yet so fair?

A/JULIET: I dunno, just lucky I guess—

D/ROMEO: Shall I believe that unsubstantial death
Is amorous, to keep thee here in the dark
To be his paramour? Here's to my love.

[*He drinks from his poison bottle.*]

O true apothecary, thy drugs are quick.
Thus, with a kiss, I die ...

[*Just as* DANIEL *leans in to kiss* ADAM, ADAM *burps. This time it is* DANIEL *who has no wish to kiss* ADAM. *He struggles with the problem for a moment, takes another swig of poison for fortification, and finally kisses him.*]

D/ROMEO: Thus with a kiss, I die.

[ROMEO *dies.* JULIET *wakes up, stretches, scratches her butt, and looks around.*]

A/JULIET: Good morning. Where, O where is my love?

[*She sees him lying at her feet and screams.*]

"What's this? A cup, closed in my true love's hand?
Poison I see hath been his timeless end. O churl.
Drunk all and left no friendly drop to help me after?
Then I'll be brief. O happy dagger! This is thy sheath."

[*She unsheathes* ROMEO'S *dagger and does a doubletake: the blade is tiny.*] That's Romeo for ya.

[*She stabs herself. She screams, but, to her surprise, she does not die. She looks for a wound and can't find one. Finally she realizes that the blade is retractable. This is a cause for much joy. She stabs herself gleefully in the torso and on the crown of the head, delighting in a variety of death noises. Finally, she flings her happy dagger to the ground.*] "There rust and let me die!" The end! [*Dies.*]

[DANIEL *and* ADAM *rise and bow.* JESS *fetches a guitar and a recorder from backstage. He hands the recorder to* DANIEL *and throws the guitar to* ADAM.]

JESS: Epilogue.

[ADAM *and* DANIEL *play a theme as* JESS *recites the epilogue.*]

JESS: "A glooming peace this morning with it brings;
The sun for sorrow will not show its head;
Go forth and have more talk of these sad things;
Some shall be pardon'd, and some punished;
For never was there a story of more woe
Than this of Juliet and her Romeo."

ALL: [*Singing.*] And Romeo and Juliet are dead.

[ADAM *and* DANIEL *rock out, jamming a power-chord rock 'n' roll coda, ending with all three doing a synchronized Pete Townshend-style jump on the last chord.*]

JESS: Thank you, Wembley, and good night!

[*Blackout. Lights come back up to reveal* DANIEL *alone onstage. The narrator's set has been struck.*]

DANIEL: Ladies and gentlemen, in preparing this unprecedented *Complete Works* show, we have encountered this problem: How to make these musty 400-year-old plays accessible to a modern audience. One popular trend is to take Shakespeare's plays and transpose them into modern settings. We have seen evidence of this with Shakespeare's plays set in such bizarre locations as the lunar landscape, Nazi concentration camps, and even New Jersey. In this vein, Jess has traced the roots of Shakespeare's symbolism in the context of a pre-Nietzschean society through the totality of a jejune circular relationship of form, contrasted with a complete otherness of metaphysical cosmologies, and the ethical mores entrenched in the collective subconscious of an agrarian race. So we now present Shakespeare's first tragedy, *Titus Andronicus*, as a cooking show.

[*A brief, cheesy musical sting brings on* JESS *as* TITUS ANDRONICUS, *wearing an apron and carrying a large meat cleaver. He has a bloody stump where his right hand should be. He is somewhat reminiscent of Julia Child.*]

J/TITUS: Good evening, everyone! Good evening, gore-mets, and welcome to 'Roman Meals.' I'm your host, Titus Androgynous. Now, when you've had a long day—your right hand chopped off, your sons murdered, your daughter raped, her tongue cut out, and both her hands chopped off—well, the last thing you want to do is cook. Unless, of course, you cook the rapist and serve him to his mother at a dinner party! My daughter Lavinia and I will show you how.

[ADAM *enters as* LAVINIA, *clutching a large mixing bowl held between her two stumps, pushing* DANIEL *as the* RAPIST *in front of her. The* RAPIST *wears a puffy red hat.*]

J/TITUS: Good evening, Lavinia!

A/LAVINIA: Ood ebeie, mubba.

J/TITUS: And how are we feeling today?

A/LAVINIA: Ot so ood, mubba. I ot my ongue yopped off.

J/TITUS: I know. It's a pisser. But we'll get our revenge, won't we?

> "Now hark, villain. I will grind your bones to dust,
> And of your blood and it I'll make a paste;
> And of the paste a coffin I will rear
> And make a pasty of your shameful head.

> [TITUS *roughly pushes the* RAPIST *to his knees, back to the audience.*]

J/TITUS: Come, Lavinia, receive the blood."

> [LAVINIA *holds the bowl under the* RAPIST'S *throat.*]

J/TITUS: First of all, we want to make a nice, clean incision from carotid artery to jugular vein, [*Slicing* RAPIST'S *throat.*] like so.

RAPIST: Aaaaargh!

A/LAVINIA: Yecch. That's weally gwoss, mubba.

> [*The* RAPIST *bows his head over the translucent bowl, dropping his red hat into it. The bowl now appears to be filled with blood.* LAVINIA *shows it to the audience cheerily.*]

J/TITUS: Be sure to use a big bowl for this because the human body has about four quarts of blood in it! "And when that he is dead," which should be ...

> [*The* RAPIST *collapses to the floor in a heap.* LAVINIA *exits.*]

J/TITUS: ... right about now,

> "let me go grind his bones to powder small
> And with this hateful liquor temper it;
> And in that paste let his vile head be baked ..."

At about 350 degrees. And 40 minutes later, you have this lovely human head pie ...

[LAVINIA *re-enters with a truly disgusting human-head pie.*]

J/TITUS: ... which I prepared earlier ... [*Pulling a severed hand from the pie.*] with—serving suggestion!—ladyfingers for dessert! Now, who will be the first to try this delicious taste treat?

[TITUS *and* LAVINIA *offer the pie to a couple in the audience.*]

J/TITUS: "Welcome, gracious lord. Welcome, dread queen. Will't please you eat? Will't please you feed?"
It's finger-lickin' good!

[JESS *and* ADAM *are excited by the clever line. They try to give each other a high-five, but since neither has a hand, it is a miserable failure.* LAVINIA *exits.*]

J/TITUS: Well, we're just about out of time, everyone. Thanks for tuning in, and be sure to watch next week, when our guest chef, Timon of Athens, will teach us how to make ratatouille out of our special guests, the Merry Wives of Windsor! Until then ...

[LAVINIA *re-enters, carrying a human femur bone.*]

J/TITUS AND A/LAVINIA: Bone appètit!

[TITUS *and* LAVINIA *exit to a musical outro sting. Blackout. Lights come back up to reveal* DANIEL.]

DANIEL: I hope no one was too offended by *Titus Andronicus*. Shakespeare as a young writer seems to have gone through an early blood and guts period. No doubt, if he were alive today he'd be in Hollywood working on *Titus Andronicus IX—Just Desserts*. But we shall now move on to explore the genius evident in Shakespeare's more mature plays, as we present his dark and brooding tragedy, *Othello, the Moor of Venice*.

[DANIEL *exits.* ADAM *enters as* OTHELLO, *with plastic boats on a string draped around his neck.*]

A/OTHELLO: "Speak of me as I am; let nothing extenuate
Of one who loved not wisely, but too well:"
For never was there a story of more woe
Than this of Othello and his Desdemono.
[*He stabs himself with a tugboat.*] O, Desi!

[*He dies amid a clatter of plastic boats.* DANIEL *and* JESS *watch from the doorway in distress. They confer briefly, then enter.*]

DANIEL: [*To the light booth.*] Bob, can we have some lights please? [*Then, to audience.*] We left Adam on his own to research this play. He must have looked up 'Moor' in the dictionary and thought it was a place where you tie up boats.

JESS: Which, in this context, is totally pea-brained. In the sixteenth century the word 'moor' referred to a person of African descent.

ADAM: Oh. I feel like such a dork. [*Exits.*]

JESS: Now, ladies and gentlemen, we obviously have a little bit of a problem in performing *Othello*, because the part is written for a black man, and we're obviously not, I mean...

JESS AND DANIEL: [*Ad lib as the actors delicately fill us in on their respective ancestral make-ups.*] ...we don't really have the physical characteristics necessary to portray... yeah, like I'm a Southern California surfer dude/I'm sorta dark-skinned, but more Semitic than African, I mean...

JESS AND DANIEL: [*Simultaneously.*] We're honkies...

JESS: ...basically, is what we are. So the bottom line here is that due to physical limitations, we are unable to perform *Othello, the Moor of Venice*, so we'll move on to...

[ADAM *re-enters, sans boats.*]

ADAM: Hey you guys, come on. We can do it. Just because we're white doesn't mean we can't do *Othello*. I got an idea.

DANIEL: No, Adam...

ADAM: It's better than the boats. Really. Just kinda join in... [*He begins snapping his fingers in a rap beat.*]

Here's the story of a brother by the name of Othello
He liked white women and he liked green Jello

JESS: [*Catching on quickly.*] Oh, yeah, yeah. Uh...

And a punk named Iago who made hisself a menace
'Cos he didn't like Othello, the Moor of Venice.

ADAM: Now Othello got married to Des-demona,

JESS: But he took off for the wars and he left her alone-a.

ADAM: It was a moan-a

JESS: A groan-a

ADAM AND JESS: He left her alone-a.

DANIEL [*Finally catching on and joining in.*]: He didn't write a letter and he didn't telephone-a!

[*They all get into it, making boom-box noises and roaming the stage with hip-hop attitude. Even* BOB, *the lighting operator, gets into it, as multicolored lights begin flashing to the beat.*]

DANIEL: Now Othello loved Desi like Adonis loved Venus!

JESS: And Desi loved Othello cuz he had a big...sword!

ADAM: But Iago had a plan that was clever and slick
He was crafty

JESS: He was sly

DANIEL: He was sort of a...penis.

ADAM: He say 'I'm gonna shaft the Moor.'

DANIEL: How you gonna do it?

DANIEL AND JESS: Tell us!

ADAM: Well I know his tragic flaw is that he's

ALL: Too damn jealous!

ADAM: I need a dupe
I need a dope
I need a kind of a shmoe...

JESS: So he find a chump sucker by the name o' Cassio.

DANIEL: And he plants on him Desdemona's handkerchief,

ADAM: So Othello gets to wonderin just maybe if...
While he been out fightin

DANIEL AND ADAM: Commandin an army

JESS: Are Desi and Cass playin hide the salami?
[*Scratching.*] Sa-sa-sa-salam
Salaaammii!

DANIEL: So he come back home an he smother the bitch

JESS: An' he thinks he pulled it off, without a hitch.

ADAM: But there's Emilia at the door

JESS: Who we met in Act Four

DANIEL: Who say, 'You big dummy, she weren't no whore.
She was

ALL: Pure

DANIEL: She was

ALL: Clean

DANIEL: She was

ALL: Virginal, too.
So why'd you have to go and make her face turn blue?

ADAM: It's true

DANIEL: It's you

ADAM AND DANIEL: Now what you gonna do?'

ADAM: And Othello say:

JESS: 'Damn, this is gettin pretty scary.'

DANIEL: So he pulled out his blade and committed hari-kari.

ADAM: Iago got caught, but he prob'ly copped a plea,

JESS: Loaded up his bags,

DANIEL: And moved to Beverly...

ALL: ...Hills, that is. [*A beat, then all three raise their fists high in a black-power salute.*] Africa!

[*The strobe effect drops out. Bows and elaborate handshakes all round.*]

DANIEL: Why don't we take a break from all this heavy tragedy and move on to the Comedies for awhile?

ADAM AND JESS: [*Ad lib.*] Yeah, great. Comedies, okay.

ALL: [*They again thrust their fists high in a black power salute.*] Comedies!

[JESS *and* ADAM *exit.*]

DANIEL: Now, when it came to the Comedies, Shakespeare was a genius at borrowing and adapting plot devices from different theatrical traditions.

[JESS *re-enters, wearing one tailcoat and carrying another which he puts on* DANIEL.]

JESS: That's right. These influences include the Roman plays of Plautus and Terence, Ovid's 'Metamorphoses,' which are hysterically funny—NOT—as well as the rich Italian tradition of Commedia Dell'Arte.

[ADAM *re-enters, wearing a tailcoat and carrying scripts, which he distributes to* DANIEL *and* JESS.]

ADAM: Yeah. Basically, Shakespeare stole everything he ever wrote.

JESS: 'Stole' is kinda strong, bro. 'Distilled,' maybe.

ADAM: Well, then he 'distilled' the three or four funniest gimmicks of his time, and milked them into sixteen plays.

DANIEL: You see, essentially Shakespeare was a formula writer. Once he found a device that worked, he used it...

ALL: Over and over and over again.

DANIEL: So, Mr. Shakespeare, the question we have is this:

ALL: Why did you write sixteen comedies when you could have written just one?

JESS: In answer to this question, we have taken the liberty of condensing all sixteen of Shakespeare's comedies into a single play, which we have entitled *The Comedy of Two Well-Measured Gentlemen Lost in the Merry Wives of Venice on a Midsummer's Twelfth Night in Winter.*

ADAM: Or...

DANIEL: *Cymbeline Taming Pericles the Merchant in the Tempest of Love As Much As You Like It For Nothing.*

ADAM: Or...

ALL: *The Love Boat Goes to Verona.*

[*Blackout. In the blackout, we hear.*]

ADAM: Comedy?

JESS: Comedy.

DANIEL: Comedy.

[*Lights come up to reveal all three actors, each in a pool of light and wearing comedy headgear.* DANIEL *wears goggles;* ADAM *wears floppy bug antennae and a clown nose;* JESS *wears a pair of Groucho Marx-funny-nose-and-glasses.*]

DANIEL: Act One. A Spanish duke swears an oath of celibacy and turns the rule of his kingdom over to his sadistic and tyrannical twin brother. He learns some fantastical feats of magic and sets sail for the Golden Age of Greece, along with his daughters, three beautiful and virginal sets of identical twins. While rounding the heel of Italy, the duke's ship is caught in a terrible tempest which, in its fury, casts the duke up on a desert island, along with the loveliest and most virginal of his daughters. This innocent vision of loveliness stumbles into a dark cave, where she is molested by an inhuman green monster who symbolizes the extreme right wing of the Republican Party.

ADAM: Act Two. The long-lost children of the duke's brother, also coincidentally three sets of identical twins, have just arrived in Italy. Though still possessed of an inner nobility, they are ragged, destitute, penniless, flea-infested shadows of the men they once were, and in the utmost extremity, are forced to borrow money from an old Jew, who deceives them into putting down their brains as collateral on the loan. Meanwhile, the six brothers fall in love with six Italian sisters, three of whom are contentious, sharp-tongued little shrews, while the other three are submissive, air-headed little bimbos.

JESS: Act Three. The shipwrecked identical daughters of the duke wash up on the shores of Italy, disguise themselves as men, and become pages to the shrews, and matchmakers to the duke's brother's sons. They lead all the lovers into a nearby forest, where, on a midsummer's night, a bunch of mischievous fairies squeeze the aphroditic juice of a hermaphroditic flower in the shrews' eyes, causing them to fall in love with their own pages, who in turn have fallen in love with the duke's brother's sons, while the 'Queen' of the 'fairies' seduces a jackass, and they all have a lovely bisexual animalistic orgy.

ALL: Act Four!

DANIEL: The elderly fathers of the Italian sisters, finding their daughters missing, dispatch messages to the pages, telling them to kill any man in the vicinity.

ADAM: However, unable to find men in the forest, the faithful messengers, in a final, misguided act of loyalty, deliver the messages to each other and kill themselves.

JESS: Meanwhile, the fish-creature and the duke arrive in the forest disguised as Russians, and for no apparent reason, perform a two-man underwater version of *Uncle Vanya*.

ALL: Act Five!

DANIEL: The duke commands the fairies to right their wrongs.

ADAM: The pages and the bimbos get into a knock-down drag-out fight in the mud...

JESS: During which the pages' clothes get ripped off, revealing female genitalia!

DANIEL: The duke recognizes his daughters!

ADAM: The duke's brother's sons recognize their uncle...

JESS: The magician turns the monster into a newt, who becomes Speaker of the House.

DANIEL: And they all get married and go out to dinner.

ADAM: Except for a minor character in the second act who gets eaten by a bear, and the duke's brother's sons who, unable to pay back the old Jew, give themselves lobotomies.

ALL: And they all live happily ever after.

[*All bow.* DANIEL *and* JESS *exit.*]

ADAM: We now move on to the rest of Shakespeare's tragedies, because basically we've found that the Comedies aren't half as funny as the Tragedies. Take for example, Shakespeare's Scottish Play, *Mac*—

[JESS *and* DANIEL *re-enter, frantically.*]

JESS AND DANIEL: [*Ad lib.*] Sssshhh! Don't talk about it in here!

ADAM: Oh, gosh, sorry. I forgot.

ALL: [*Whispering to audience.*] Which you're really not supposed to talk about in a theater unless you're performing it, because it's cursed. [*Leaping into front row, loudly.*] Booga, booga, booga!

[JESS *and* ADAM *exit.*]

DANIEL: Fortunately, however, we not only perform an abbreviated version of *Macbeth*—

[ADAM *re-enters with* DANIEL'S *witch costume, trips over his own feet and falls flat on his face. A beat as they look first at each other, then warily around the theater for possible kilted poltergeists. Then, quickly recovering.*]

DANIEL: But, after much thorough research, we are able to do so . . .

DANIEL AND ADAM: . . . in perfect Scottish accents!

[DANIEL *dons the costume and becomes the witch.* ADAM *exits.*]

D/WITCH: "Double, double, toil and trouble.

[JESS *enters as* MACBETH, *with a sword. In nearly impenetrable Scottish accents.*]

J/MACBETH: Stay, ye imperrrfect macspeaker. Mactell me macmore.

D/WITCH: Macbeth, Macbeth, beware Macduff.
None of woman born shall harm Macbeth
Till Birnam Wood come to Dunsinane, don't ye know.

[WITCH *exits.* ADAM *enters as* MACDUFF, *hiding behind a twig.*]

J/MACBETH: Och, that's dead great. Then macwhat macneed macI macfear of Macduff?

[MACDUFF *throws down his disguise, wields his sword and throws a two-fingered gesture at* MACBETH.]

A/MACDUFF: See you, Jimmy, and know
That I was from my mother's womb untimely ripped!"
What d'ye think about that?

J/MACBETH: Och! I do nae like it, but I support a woman's right t'choose! Lay on, ye great haggis-face.

[*They fence.*]

A/MACDUFF: Ah, Macbeth! Ye killed my wife, ye murdered my babies, ye shat in my stew.

J/MACBETH: Och! I didnae!

A/MACDUFF: O, ay ye did. I had t' throw half of it away.

[MACDUFF *chases* MACBETH *offstage. Backstage,* MACBETH'S *scream is abruptly cut off.* MACDUFF *re-enters carrying a severed head.*]

A/MACDUFF: Behold where lies the usurper's cursed head. Macbeth, yer arse is out the windie. [*Drop-kicks the head into the audience.*] And know,
That never was there a story o' more blood and death
Than this, o' Mr. and Mrs. Macbeth. Thankee. [*Exits.*]

[JESS *enters.*]

JESS: Meanwhile, Julius Caesar was a much-beloved tyrant.

[ADAM *enters.*]

ADAM AND JESS: [*Performing a ritualistic salute.*] All hail, Julius Caesar!

[DANIEL *enters as* JULIUS CAESAR, *wearing a laurel wreath.*]

D/CAESAR: Hail, citizens!

JESS: Who was warned by a soothsayer . . .

[ADAM *pulls his shirt over his head and becomes the* SOOTH-SAYER.]

A/SOOTHSAYER: "Beware the Ides of March."

JESS: The great Caesar, however, chose to ignore the warning.

D/CAESAR: What the hell are the Ides of March?

A/SOOTHSAYER: The 15th of March.

D/CAESAR: Why, that's today.

[JESS *and* ADAM *stab him repeatedly. He falls.* ADAM *exits.*]

D/CAESAR: "Et tu, Brute?

[CAESAR *dies.* JESS *becomes* MARK ANTONY, *orating over the body.*]

J/ANTONY: Friends, Romans, countrymen, lend me your ears. I come to bury Caesar," so bury him, and let's get on to my play,
Antony . . .

[ADAM *enters as* CLEOPATRA, *wearing a wig and clutching a rubber snake.*]

A/CLEOPATRA: . . . *and Cleopatra!* Is this an asp I see before me?

[CLEOPATRA *applies the snake to her breast, and immediately vomits on several people in the front row.*]

JESS AND DANIEL: Whoa, Adam! No! Stop!

ADAM: What?

DANIEL: You have this bizarre notion that all of Shakespeare's tragic heroines wear really ugly wigs and vomit on people before they die.

ADAM: Well . . . don't they?

JESS: No, no—get a clue, bro! *Antony and Cleopatra* is not a Pepto-Bismol commercial. It's a romantic thriller about a geopolitical power struggle between Egypt and Rome.

ADAM: Oh, it's one of Shakespeare's geopolitical plays? Wow, if I'd known that I'd never have screwed around with it, 'cuz Shakespeare's geopolitical work is my favorite stuff. It's like, the themes he wrote about four hundred years ago are still relevant today. Like, what was that one he wrote about how nuclear energy affected the Soviet Union?

JESS: Adam, Shakespeare never wrote anything about the Soviet Union.

ADAM: Yeah, he totally did. It was called *Chernobyl Kinsmen*, and it was intense. It's about this nuclear reactor that melts down and pollutes the air and water of all the neighboring kingdoms, but the king of Chernobyl denies that it ever happened, even though the peasants are, like, growing second heads and stuff. Then in the second act, this radioactive cloud floats over to the New World, and it creates this genetically mutated race of TV evangelists—

DANIEL: Adam, what are you talking about?

ADAM: *Chernobyl Kinsmen*, it was—

DANIEL: No, Adam. Shakespeare wrote a play called *Two Noble Kinsmen*.

JESS: Not *Chernobyl Kinsmen*!

DANIEL: *Two Noble Kinsmen*.

ADAM: Oh. What's *Two Noble Kinsmen* about?

JESS: It's about a girl who goes insane with the fear that her boyfriend is going to be eaten by wolves and her father hanged.

ADAM: And is there anything in it about Boris Yeltsin?

JESS AND DANIEL: No.

ADAM: Well, I've never even heard of that play.

JESS: I'm not surprised you haven't heard of it, because it's not actually... hmm. Maybe I should explain. [*To the audience.*] Ladies and gentlemen, *Two Noble Kinsmen* actually falls into the category of Shakespeare's plays which scholars refer to as *The Apocryhpha*, or in some scholarly circles, *The Obscure Plays*, or *The Lesser Plays*, or simply, *The Bad Plays*. And yet, not all of The Apocryhpha are completely without merit. In fact, one of them, *Troilus and Cressida*, is hardly crap at all. [*He's becoming excited with the breadth of his own scholarly achievement now.*] I actually discuss it at some length in my soon-to-be-released book about Shakespeare, entitled *I Love My Willy*, which I'd like to whip out for you now.

DANIEL AND ADAM: Jess, no, not here!

JESS: [*Reaching into his pants and extracting... a manuscript. To* DANIEL *and* ADAM.] The manuscript, guys... I was thinking that maybe tonight we could do a kind of a quick improvised version of *Troilus and Cressida* based on this chapter.

DANIEL: Yeah! We could do an interpretive dance/performance art version!

ADAM: Oh, I love performance art. It's so... [*Searching for the word.*] ... pretentious! We could use *Troilus and Cressida* as a jumping-off point to explore deeper themes like the transient nature of life and the mythology involved in the arising and dissipation of forms.

DANIEL: Yeah, get some props!

JESS: Now wait just a minute. I was actually thinking of a straightforward, scholarly approach—

ADAM: Naw, screw that. [*He exits.*]

DANIEL: Go ahead and read. [*He poses.*]

JESS: Well, okay. '*Troilus and Cressida* was written in 1603, published in quarto in 1604, and appears in the First Folio, although this version is some 166 lines longer than the second quarto edition of 1645, which is some 166 lines shorter.'

[DANIEL *performs an awkward dance-mime as* ADAM *re-enters, first with an inflatable dinosaur and then with a battery-operated Godzilla that walks and roars.* DANIEL *and* JESS *stare at the scourge of Tokyo, and then at* ADAM, *until he turns it off and exits like a wounded puppy dog, taking his toy with him.*]

JESS: Ladies and gentlemen, my book has nothing to do with Godzilla. It discusses the possibility that Shakespeare's plays were actually written by a monkey at a typewriter. I think it's groundbreaking work, and—

DANIEL: Wait a minute. Isn't there something in there about the plot?

[ADAM *re-enters with a crown.*]

JESS: Plot? Of course I cover the plot. What kind of scholar do you think I am? I cover the plot in depth in the footnote on page twenty-nine. [*Reading.*] 'Troilus, youngest son of Priam, King of Troy...'

ADAM: Okay, you be Troilus and you [*Crowning* JESS.] be the King.

JESS: Okay, great. '...loves Cressida...'

[JESS *and* DANIEL *look at* ADAM.]

ADAM: I'll get the wig. [ADAM *exits, fetches the wig and re-enters.*]

JESS: '...and has arranged with her uncle Pandarus for a meeting. Although she feigns indifference, she is attracted to him...'

ADAM: I have to feign indifference?!

JESS: Yeah! '... meanwhile, Agamemnon, the Greek commander, has surrounded the Trojans—'

ADAM AND DANIEL: Agamemnon?!? Jess, this is boring, boring, boring!

DANIEL: This is the kind of stuff that kids hate to study in school because it's so boring.

ADAM: Yeah, like as soon as you said 'Agamemnon,' I was asleep. No, I'm sorry [*To audience.*], I told these guys backstage, right before we went on, I told them, 'I will NOT do dry, boring... vomitless Shakespeare for these people,' because it'll just turn you off to Shakespeare. I mean, that's what happened to me. When I was a kid I used to sit there in class, and while we were supposed to be studying Shakespeare, I'd be looking out the window at all the kids playing ball, and I'd be thinking to myself, 'Why can't this Shakespeare stuff be more like sports?'

JESS: Sports?

DANIEL: How do you mean?

ADAM: Well, sports are visceral, they're exciting to watch. I mean, take the histories, for example. With all those kings and queens killing each other off, and the throne passing from one generation to the next... it's exactly like playing football, but you do it with a crown.

JESS: Hey, they are kinda similar, aren't they?

DANIEL: Yeah, I can see that. Okay, line 'em up. Let's kick some royal ass!

[*They line up in a three-man football formation. Then, like a quarterback calling signals.*]

DANIEL: Twenty-five!... Forty-two... Richard the Third... Henry the Sixth, Part One! Two! Three...

ALL: HUP!

JESS: [*Like a football announcer.*] . . . and the crown is snapped to Richard the Second, that well-spoken fourteenth-century monarch. He's fading back to pass, looking for an heir downfield, but there's a heavy rush from King John.

[JESS, *as* KING JOHN, *stabs* DANIEL, *who flings the crown into the air as he croaks.*]

D/RICHARD II: "My gross flesh sinks downwards!"

JESS: The crown is in the air, and Henry the Sixth comes up with it!

A/HENRY VI: [*Catches and dons the crown.*] Victory is mine!

DANIEL: [*Announcer.*] But he's hit immediately by King John, that rarely performed player from the twelfth century, and he's down.

[KING JOHN *begins stabbing the fallen* HENRY VI *repeatedly.*]

DANIEL: Ooh, he's killin' him out there! This could be the end of the War of the Roses cycle!

[KING JOHN *grabs the crown from the now-dead* HENRYVI *and takes off running.*]

ADAM: [*Announcer.*] King John is in the clear . . .

J/KING JOHN: "My soul hath elbow room!"

[DANIEL *grabs the poison bottle, still onstage from* JULIET'S *death scene, and pours poison down* KING JOHN'S *throat.*]

ADAM: He's at the forty, the thirty, the twenty—he's poisoned on the ten yard line!

[JESS *exits, as* DANIEL *takes the crown and becomes* KING LEAR.]

ADAM: Looks like he's out for the game. Replacing him now is number seventy-two, King Lear.

D/KING LEAR: [*Drawing a play on his hand.*] "Divide we our kingdom in three." Cordelia, you go long...

[JESS *re-enters, throws a penalty marker and whistles play dead.*]

ADAM: A penalty marker is down.

[JESS *makes a hand signal and points at* LEAR.]

ADAM: Fictional character on the field. Lear is disqualified, and he's not happy about it.

D/KING LEAR: Puckey!

[LEAR *hands over the crown with disgust, and we begin a new play.* JESS *as* HENRY IV *at center,* ADAM *as* PRINCE HAL *at quarterback,* DANIEL *as* RICHARD III *at halfback.*]

ADAM: Lining up now is that father-son team of Henry the Fourth and Prince Hal. Center snaps to the quarterback... quarterback gives to the hunchback. It looks like Richard the Third's limp is giving him trouble.

D/RICHARD III: "A horse, a horse! My kingdom for a horse!"

[*A massive crunch as* RICHARD III *goes down, and* JESS *and the dummy pile on top.*]

ADAM: There's a pile-up on the field.

[*The crown rolls from the prone* RICHARD III *to* ADAM, *who becomes* HENRY IV. *He takes off running toward the end zone.*]

DANIEL: [*Announcer.*] FUM-BLE!!! And Henry the Eighth comes up with it. He's at the twenty, the fifteen, the ten... he stops at the five to chop off his wife's head... TOUCHDOWN for the Red Rose! Oh, my! You gotta believe this is the beginning of a Tudor Dynasty!

[*They all line up as cheerleaders, and perform a perky little routine.*]

ALL/CHEERLEADERS: Henry the Fifth, Richard the Third, the whole royal family's friggin' absurd! Especially CHARLES! Yay!

[DANIEL *and* JESS *congratulate each other as* ADAM *clambers into the audience.*]

ADAM: Can I have some house lights please? [*To an audience member.*] Can I borrow your program for a sec? [*He grabs a program from a patron.*]

DANIEL: What are you doing?

ADAM: I just want to check the list of plays. I think we might have done 'em all already.

JESS: Really?

ADAM: Yeah. [*To audience.*] We might be able to let you out a little early tonight.

JESS: That'd be great.

[*They consult the list of plays in the program NOTE: if there is no list of plays in the program, they can consult the* Complete Works *book.*]

ADAM: Because, see, we did all the Histories just now—

DANIEL: And we covered the Comedies in a lump—

JESS: Okay, that leaves the Tragedies. We did *Titus Andronicus* with all the blood—

ADAM: *Romeo and Juliet* we did—

DANIEL: *Julius Caesar, Troilus and Cressida*, right—

JESS: We rapped *Othello*, and Lear was in the football game, *Macbeth* we did with Scottish accents. What about *Antony and Cleopatra*?

ADAM: Yeah, I vomited on that lady over there—

JESS: Right. *Timon of Athens* I mentioned. *Coriolanus*?

ADAM: I don't want to do that one.

DANIEL: Why? What's the matter with *Coriolanus*?

ADAM: I don't like the 'anus' part. I think it's offensive.

JESS: Okay, so we skip the anus play.

DANIEL: And that's it, right? That's all of them.

JESS: Hey, you guys . . . [*Points to a spot in the program.*]

ALL: Oh, no. *Hamlet!*

JESS: How could we forget *Hamlet?*

DANIEL: I dunno. It's right there.

ADAM: Shakespeare didn't write *Hamlet*, did he?

JESS: Of course he did.

ADAM: I thought it was a Mel Gibson movie.

JESS: Ladies and gentlemen, thirty-six plays down, one to go. Perhaps the greatest play ever written in the English language. A play of such lofty poetic and philo—

[ADAM *tugging at* JESS'S *sleeve.*]

ADAM: Wait a minute, Jess. *Hamlet* is a really serious, hard-core play, and I'm just not up for it right now.

JESS: Whaddaya mean? It's the last one. We've done thirty-six already!

ADAM: I know. It's just that that football game left me emotionally and physically drained, and I just don't think that I could do it justice.

JESS: We don't have to do it justice. We just have to do it.

ADAM: [*Slinking into audience.*] I don't wanna do it!

DANIEL: Look, Adam. Our show's called *The Complete Works of William Shakespeare.* [*Indicating audience.*] I think they'd like to see *Hamlet.*

ADAM: Okay, so we'll call it *The Complete Works of William Shakespeare Except Hamlet.*

JESS: [*Following* ADAM *into audience.*] That's the most ridiculous thing I've ever heard!

ADAM: Well if YOU wanna do it, then go ahead and do it. I don't have to if I don't want to. I'll just sit here with this lady. [*Sits on an audience member's lap.*] She's my friend. I'll sit here and watch you two do it.

DANIEL: C'mon. Adam—

[JESS *and* DANIEL *try to pry him loose from the audience member, but* ADAM *starts to get hysterical.*]

ADAM: You can't make me do it! You can't!

JESS: [*To audience member.*] Hey! Leggo of our actor!

ADAM: Okay, okay! Just don't touch me.

DANIEL: Are you alright?

ADAM: I'm fine.

JESS: We're going to do *Hamlet* now, right?

ADAM: Yeah.

JESS: Okay. Geez, have a cow!

[*Tosses a now-crumpled wad back to the audience member.*] Here's your program back. Sorry, it got kinda trashed. [*To* DANIEL.] Right. We start off with the guard scene, so we need Bernardo and Horatio.

DANIEL: We'll need Rosencrantz and Guildenstern.

JESS: Nah, they've got their own play, we can skip them.

[*While* JESS *is distracted,* ADAM *sprints toward the exit at the back of the theater.*]

JESS: Hey, where do you think you're going?!

[JESS *sprints after him.* ADAM *sees he's being chased and grabs an audience member as a hostage.*]

ADAM: I'll kill this guy! I'll kill him!

JESS: You leave him alone!

[ADAM *lets go of his victim and darts for the door.*]

JESS: Get back here this instant, you Shakespeare wimp!!

[ADAM *runs out the back of the house.* JESS *follows, slamming the door behind him. We hear* ADAM *scream once in the lobby, and then silence. They are gone.* DANIEL *follows them a little way up the aisle, then stops. The house lights dim as he returns to the stage ... suddenly and conspicuously alone.*]

DANIEL: Jess is usually much faster than Adam. I'm sure they'll be right back. [DANIEL *stalls for awhile, doing whatever he can to entertain the audience. Tells jokes. Does impressions. As long as it's funny. And slightly pathetic. Then, just when it's gone on almost a little bit too long ...*]

Why don't we take the intermission here. Go out to the lobby, stretch your legs, get something to drink; we're always much funnier after you've had a couple of drinks. I'll meet you back here in fifteen minutes. Adam and Jess should be back by then, and we will proceed with *Hamlet, Prince of Denmark*—I hope.

[DANIEL *exits. Lights come up in the house. Halftime music kicks in. A roller-skating prop mistress rolls out onstage and begins to pick up props littered around the stage. It's ...*]

Intermission

ACT TWO

The intermission music fades out and lights come up—on an empty stage. After a beat, DANIEL *enters nervously, costumed as* HORATIO *for the opening of* Hamlet.

DANIEL: [*To audience.*] Hi. [*He waits for a response, then.*] Have a nice intermission? [*He again waits for a response.*] Yeah? What'd you do? [*He waits for a response.*] Was there a long line at the Ladies' room? [*Of course there was.*] Yeah, I hate that. Um, Jess and Adam aren't back yet. Actually, Jess called during the intermission. He found Adam at the airport, trying to catch a flight out of here. He said until they got back, I should cover the sonnets. [*Pause.*] Shakespeare wrote one hundred and fifty-four sonnets. I've condensed them down onto this three-by-five card [*He produces one.*], and I was thinking maybe what we could do is pass it among the audience. Like if we start right here with you [*Indicating a member of the audience.*]; you take it, read it, enjoy it, then pass it to the person next to you, and so on down the row, and then you pass it behind you, and so on, back and forth and back and forth and back and forth. And back and forth and back and forth and back, and by the time it gets to you [*In the back.*] Jess and Adam should be here. So if we could have some house lights here . . . just take it, read it, pass it to the person next to you.

[DANIEL *hands the card to the patron. He produces his recorder and plays the theme from 'Jeopardy' for a bar or two, until he's interrupted by a commotion a the back of the house:* JESS *entering, dragging the still-unwilling* ADAM *behind him.*]

DANIEL: Jess and Adam, ladies and gentlemen!

[JESS *drags* ADAM *to the stage.*]

JESS: Sorry it took so long . . .

ADAM: [*Crying.*] I don't wanna do it. It's just so big. It's got so many words . . .

JESS: We can do it, man. We know *Hamlet* backwards and forwards.

[ADAM *begins to hack and cough.*]

JESS: Oh, not this again! [*Holds up his shirt for* ADAM *to honk his nose into.*] Here, Adam. Blow. Blow!

[*He does.*]

JESS: Daniel, take him backstage and get him together. I'll take the intro out here.

[DANIEL *and* ADAM *exit.* JESS *looks at the snot in his shirt.*]

JESS: I bet Laurence Olivier doesn't have to do this. Well, not anymore, anyway. [*To light booth.*] Bob, can I have a little bit of mood lighting out here please, to set the scene for perhaps the greatest play ever written in the English language?

[BOB *accommodates with a bored 'Yeah, okay.' The lights change to a cold midnight blue, dappled with moonlight.*]

JESS: *Hamlet, the Tragedy of the Prince of Denmark!* The place: Denmark. The time: The twelfth, maybe the thirteenth century, give or take. The battlements of Elsinore castle, round about midnight. Two guards enter.

   [*Exits. After a beat, we hear from offstage, sotto voce.*] Well, go on, Adam. Get out there.

ADAM: [*O.S.*] No. I don't wanna.

JESS: [*O.S.*] C'mon, you said you would.

ADAM: [*O.S.*] No, no, no . . .

[*The escalating backstage argument is cut off by the abrupt sound of a slap, followed by the sound of* ADAM *blowing his nose.* ADAM *enters as* BERNARDO, *wiping his nose;* DANIEL *enters opposite as* HORATIO.]

A/BERNARDO: "Who's there?

D/HORATIO: Nay, answer me. Stand and unfold yourself.

A/BERNARDO: Long live the King.

D/HORATIO: Bernardo?

A/BERNARDO: He. 'Tis now struck twelve. Get thee to bed, Horatio.

D/HORATIO: For this relief, much thanks.

A/BERNARDO: Well, good night.

D/HORATIO: Peace, break thee off. Look where it comes!

[*The* GHOST *of* HAMLET'S *father enters. Well, it's actually just a sweat sock with a big happy face drawn on it, dangling from a fishing line upstage center. But it's ver-ry scar-ry nevertheless.* JESS *makes ghostly moaning sounds from backstage.*]

A/BERNARDO: Mark it, Horatio. It would be spoke to.

D/HORATIO: What art thou? By heaven, I charge thee, speak!

[JESS *makes the sound of a cock crowing, and the sock disappears.*]

  'Tis gone.

A/BERNARDO: It was about to speak when the cock crew.

D/HORATIO: Break we our watch up; and by my advice, let us impart what we have seen tonight unto ...

BOTH: Hamlet, Prince of Denmark!

[*They exit together. Lights change back to a day wash.* JESS *enters as* HAMLET. *He is classically costumed: black tights, black pants, black doublet, black hat, and dagger. But he's still wearin' those Converse Chuck Taylors ...*]

J/HAMLET: [*Oh-so dramatic.*] O that this too too solid flesh would melt,
  Thaw, and resolve itself into a dew.

That it should come to this, but two months dead.
So loving to my mother.

[*Points to a woman in the audience.*]

Frailty, thy name is woman. Yeah, you!
Married with mine uncle, my father's brother.
Thy funeral baked meats did coldly furnish forth
The marriage tables.

[*He kneels and begins sobbing uncontrollably; a very impressive display of melancholy, a performance that William Shatner... er, Shakespeare...himself would be proud of. HORATIO and BERNARDO appear in the up left doorway, and watch HAMLET bawl. BERNARDO nods for HORATIO to approach him. HORATIO enters as BERNARDO disappears.*]

D/HORATIO: My lord!

J/HAMLET: Horatio!

[*They exchange a very silly Wittenberg University Danish Club handshake.*]

J/HAMLET: Methinks I see my father.

D/HORATIO: Where, my lord?

J/HAMLET: In my mind's eye, Horatio.

D/HORATIO: My lord, I think I saw him yesternight.

J/HAMLET: Saw who?

D/HORATIO: The king, your father.

J/HAMLET: The king my father? But where was this?

D/HORATIO: Upon the platform where we watched.

J/HAMLET: 'Tis very strange. I will watch tonight.
Perchance 'twill walk again. All is not well.
Would the night were come.

[*The stage lighting changes suddenly back to night. The quick change catches* JESS *and* DANIEL *off guard. They give a thumbs-up to the light booth, and commence acting cold.*]

J/HAMLET: The air bites shrewdly. It is very cold.

D/HORATIO: Look, my lord, it comes!

J/HAMLET: Angels and ministers of grace defend us. Something is rotten in the state of Denmark.

[ADAM *enters as the* GHOST *of* HAMLET'S *father. He wears a ghostly robe that is somewhat reminiscent of a sweat sock, but his voice is more along the lines of Bela Lugosi.*]

A/GHOST: Mark me!

J/HAMLET: Speak. I am bound to hear.

A/GHOST: So art thou to revenge when thou shalt hear. If ever thou didst thy dear father love Revenge his foul and most unnatural murther.

J/HAMLET: Murther!

D/HORATIO: Murther!

A/GHOST: The serpent that did sting thy father's life Now wears his crown.

J/HAMLET: My uncle.

D/HORATIO: Your uncle!

A/GHOST: Let not the royal bed of Denmark Become a couch for incest.

J/HAMLET: Incest!

D/HORATIO: A couch!

A/GHOST: Adieu, Hamlet, remember me! [*Exits.*]

D/HORATIO: My lord, this is strange.

J/HAMLET: There are more things in heaven and earth, Horatio,

Than are dreamt of in your philosophy. So... [*Slapping him.*] piss off.

[HORATIO *exits.*]

J/HAMLET: I hereafter shall think meet to put an antic disposition on.
The time is out of joint. O cursed spite that ever I was born to exit right.

[HAMLET *tries to 'exit right' but smashes into the proscenium arch, falls down, gets up. He exits, we hear a crash in the wings, a roller skate rolls onstage and out the upstage left door.* DANIEL *enters as* POLONIUS. *He watches the roller skate go offstage. He is a doddering old man. He takes his time, totters slowly downstage centers, adjusts his dentures, clears his throat, and...*]

D/POLONIUS: Neither a borrower nor a lender be.

[*He is tremendously satisfied with himself. He turns and waddles toward the upstage right door, where he is run over by* ADAM *entering screaming as* OPHELIA. *It is a very, very, very lengthy scream.*]

A/OPHELIA: [*One breath.*] Aaaaaaaaaaaaaaaaaaaaauuuuuuugh!

D/POLONIUS: How now, Ophelia, what's the matter?

A/OPHELIA: [*Breathless.*] My lord, as I was sewing in my closet,
Lord Hamlet, with his doublet all unbraced,
No hat upon his head, pale as his shirt,
His knees knocking each other, and with a look
So piteous in purport as if he had been loosed
Out of hell to speak of horrors... [*Fraught with meaning.*] he comes before me.

D/POLONIUS: Mad for thy love?

A/OPHELIA: [*After another very lengthy scream.*]
Aaaaaaaaaaaaauuuuuuugggh.
I know not.

D/POLONIUS: Why, this is the very ecstasy of love.
I have found the cause of Hamlet's lunacy.
Since brevity is the soul of wit, I will be brief:
He is mad.

[HAMLET *enters reading a book, feigning madness. Actually, he's completely off-the-wall bonkers, doing a Monty-Python-esque silly walk.*]

D/POLONIUS: Look you where the poor wretch comes reading.
Away, I do beseech you.

[OPHELIA *exits.*]

D/POLONIUS: How does my good lord Hamlet?

J/HAMLET: Well, God-a-mercy.

D/POLONIUS: Do you know me my lord?

J/HAMLET: Excellent well. You are a fishmonger.

D/POLONIUS: What do you read, my lord?

J/HAMLET: Words, words, words.

D/POLONIUS: [*Aside.*] Though this be madness, yet there's method in't."

A/OPHELIA: [*Poking her head out from backstage.*] Daddy, the Players are here and they want to talk to you right away so you'd better get back here as soon as you can cuz they want something I dunno what they want but you'd better hurry…

[*She disappears.* POLONIUS *follows her off.*]

J/HAMLET: [*Suddenly serious, intense.*]
"I am but mad north-northwest. When the wind is
  southerly,
I know a hawk from a handsaw.
I'll have these players play something like
The murder of my father before mine uncle.
I'll observe his looks. If he do but blench,

I know my course. The play's the thing
Wherein I'll catch the conscience of the king!

[HAMLET *drops dramatically to one knee as the lights change to a single dramatic spotlight. Only problem is, he missed his mark badly, and is out of the light. Still on one knee, he shuffles into the light. He draws his dagger; with increasing intensity.*]

To be, or not to be? That is the question.
Whether 'tis nobler in the mind to suffer
The slings and arrows of outrageous fortune
Or to take arms against a sea of troubles
And by opposing end them.

[*He's really intense now; maybe a little too intense.*] To die;
    to sleep;"

[*Hysterical.*] Or just to take a nap and hope you wake up
In time for dinner because you gotta make
Guacamole for twelve and you just can't take the pres-
    sure of this speech!!!

[JESS *collapses into a heap.* DANIEL *and* ADAM *rush in to comfort him, gesturing for more light.*]

    [*Raving.*] I can't do it!

ADAM: Jess, look, Daniel and I have been talking about it backstage, and you don't have to go on with the speech if you don't want to.

JESS: [*Small.*] I'm so embarrassed.

ADAM: Ladies and gentlemen, you'll have to excuse him. It's a very heavy emotional speech, and he's been under a lot of pressure lately, what with what happened with Felicia—

JESS: [*Raving again.*] Felicia!!!

DANIEL: Felicia is Jess's favorite character on General Hospital. He's upset because . . .

[DANIEL *updates the audience on Felicia's trauma of the day as* JESS *slowly recovers.*]

ADAM: Yeah, so I think for tonight we should just skip this speech. I'm sorry if anybody feels ripped off, but we think it's a really overrated speech anyway. I mean, Hamlet is supposed to be thinking about killing his uncle and instead he's talking about killing himself, so we feel it just weakens the character. So we'll just skip it and move on to a later point in the play—

DANIEL: Shall we skip to the play-within-a-play sequence?

ADAM: Yeah. We'll just skip ahead, so you really don't miss anything—

DANIEL: Wait a minute, there's that one other speech of Hamlet's. I don't know if we should cut it.

ADAM: Oh, the "What a piece of work is man" speech?

DANIEL: Yeah.

ADAM: Right. Well, there's this one speech that goes: "I have of late, but wherefore I know not, lost all my mirth, forgone all custom of exercise; and indeed it goes so heavy with my disposition that this goodly frame, the earth, seems to me a sterile promontory; this most excellent canopy, the air, look you; this brave o'erhanging firmament, this majestic roof fretted with golden fire, why it appears to me no more than a foul and pestilent congregation of vapours. What a piece of work is man; how noble in reason, how infinite in faculty, in form and moving how express and admirable; in action how like an angel; in apprehension how like a god. The beauty of the world, the paragon of animals; and yet to me, what is this quintessence of dust? Man delights not me."

[*He has delivered the speech simply, quietly and with barely a gesture or a trace of interpretation. You can hear a pin drop.*]

DANIEL: So we'll skip that speech and go right to the killing.

[*They all start to exit, then* DANIEL *remembers.*]

DANIEL: Wait a minute. What about the "get thee to a nunnery" scene?

JESS: Oh yeah, let's do that one real quick...

ADAM: No, we can't. I'm not in the right costume.

DANIEL: We have to. It's central to the plot.

ADAM: I can't! I'm not in the right character either. Ophelia is a very difficult and complex character.

DANIEL: No, it's easy.

ADAM: It's not.

DANIEL: It is. Anybody could play that character. My mother could play that character. That lady right there [*Pointing to a woman in the audience.*] could play that character.

JESS: Well, let's get her to do it then. This is giving me a headache...

[JESS *and* DANIEL *go and grab the* 'VOLUNTEER' *from the audience, and bring her onstage. NOTE: this is an actual member of the audience, NOT a plant!*]

ADAM: You guys, this isn't fair. C'mon, Jess, I didn't make you do your speech. You can't just bring some bozo onstage to play Ophelia!

JESS: She's not a bozo, and besides, she volunteered.
[*To* VOLUNTEER.] Okay, first of all, what's your name?

[*She responds.*]

JESS: Do you mind if we call you 'Bob?' It's a little easier to remember. Okay, Bob, this is a very simple scene—

ADAM: It's extremely difficult.

JESS: Hamlet has had this relationship with Ophelia, but what with what's been happening with his father and his mother and his uncle and yatta-yatta-yatta, he can't deal with her anymore—

ADAM: He's being a prick.

JESS: So he gets all worked up and tells her to get out of his life. He says, "Get thee to a nunnery." Now in our version of this scene, all that Ophelia does in response is, she screams.
    [*Pointedly, to* ADAM.] That's all she does. Hamlet says, "Get thee to a nunnery," and Ophelia screams. Okay? Let's give it a try.

ADAM: [*Shoving her slightly as he crosses past her.*] Good luck.

[*A brief pause while* JESS *prepares, then.*]

JESS: "Get thee to a nunnery!"

[*The* VOLUNTEER *screams—probably not very well.*]

DANIEL: Did you hear that, Adam? I thought it was really good.

JESS: It was okay.

ADAM: No, it sucked, really. I mean, I don't mean to be catty, but you're not an actress, and frankly, it shows. You obviously had no idea what was going on inside Ophelia's head.

JESS: Actors use what they call 'subtext,' Bob.

DANIEL: Or 'inner monologue.'

ADAM: Exactly. That's what you didn't have, and as a result your performance was just flat and one-dimensional. But I think you showed a lot of heart. A lot of courage. A lot of—as Shakespeare would say—'chutzpah,' and I think we should WORKSHOP this. I think we could really make this a happening moment. In fact [*To the light booth.*], Bob? Could you bring up the house lights, please?

[*The house lights come up. During the following, and up until the second scream,* DANIEL *quietly and unobtrusively coaches the* VOLUNTEER *whenever he can, making it clear to her that the entire second act of the show rises or falls on the power and vehemence of her second scream: 'Take a deep breath, keep your head up, and belt out a LONG, LOUD scream right to the very back of the theater. LOUD and LONG! LONG and LOUD!'.*]

ADAM: [*Cont'd to audience.*] Cuz I think we should get everybody involved in this. You know, sort of create a supportive environment for Bob here [*Indicating the* VOLUNTEER.]. Maybe we could get everybody to act out what's going on inside of Ophelia's head. Like, divide everybody up into Ophelia's Id, Ego, and Superego—

JESS: Oh yeah, like a Freudian analysis!

ADAM: Yeah, a Floydian analysis!

DANIEL: I get the Id!

JESS: Cool! I'll get the Ego.

[JESS *grabs a guy out of the audience—also NOT a plant—and hustles him up onstage.*]

ADAM: Now you're playing the part of Ophelia's ego. At this point in the play her ego is flighty, it's confused...it's an Ego on the run.

JESS: Oh, great! So we'd like you to symbolize this, Bob, by—oh, do you mind if we call you 'Bob?'—we'll symbolize this by actually having you run back and forth across the stage in front of Ophelia. Will you give that a try? Right now, just...

ALL: Go, go, go, go, go, go!

[*The* EGO *runs back and forth across the stage.*]

DANIEL: Wow. A little bit of an ego-maniac! Okay, now everyone in the front three rows, you're going to be Ophelia's Id. Her Id is confused, it's wishy-washy, it's awash in a sea of alternatives. So everybody, hands in the air, wave them back and forth, kind of undulate, and say, [*In falsetto.*] 'Maybe...maybe not...maybe...maybe not.' Okay, that's good. Save some for later.

JESS: [*Picking on a less-than-enthusiastic member of the Id.*] Right. What was your problem? YOU were not participating with the rest of the group. You know what that means, don't you? You're going to have to do it—

ALL: ALL...BY...YOUR...SELF.

DANIEL: Don't be embarrassed, nobody's watching.

[*They make the malingerer do it alone.*]

ADAM: I dunno, I feel a lot of love in this room. Now why don't we get everybody behind the front three rows to be Ophelia's Superego. This is the final psychological component. The Superego is made up of those strong, moralistic voices inside your head that tell you exactly what to do. They're very powerful, very difficult to shake. Some people never shake them in their whole lifetime...sorta like Catholicism. It's a very complex part of the psyche, so— Jess, why dontcha help me out on this.

JESS: [*Drawing out his dagger.*] Okay.

ADAM: Why don't we divide the Superego into three parts? Let's have everybody from where Jess is indicating...

[JESS, *indicating with his dagger, slices off the left third of the audience.*]

ADAM: [*Cont'd.*]to my left be Section 'A.' Everyone from Jess to here [*Indicating the middle third of the audience.*], you're Section 'B.' And everyone from here over to my right, you're section . . . ? [*He prompts the audience to respond. They call out, 'C'.*] Yeah, it's not too bloody difficult, is it?

[*NOTE: Section B should actually be just slightly larger than Sections A and C.*]

Now section A is the masculine part of Ophelia's brain, the animus, so to speak. And I'd like you to use Hamlet's line for this. I'd like you to say, "Get thee to a nunnery!" Let's try it. Section A?

[*They respond.*]

DANIEL: Section A, that was awful.

ADAM: C'mon, people, work with me on this. We want it very loud, very strident. Section A?

[*They respond.*]

JESS: Yes! Much less totally pathetic!

ADAM: Okay, Section B. You're the voice of vanity, saying, for God's sake, do something with yourself. Put on some makeup or something—[*To the* VOLUNTEER] no offense— really, this is straight out of the Shakespearean text. [*Back to the audience.*] I'd like you all to say, "Paint an inch thick!" Section B?

[*They respond. Probably a little louder, because they're a little bigger.*]

ADAM: Oooh. Section A could learn something from Section B. Okay, now Section C, we've saved you for last because you're the most important component of them all, because we're going to use you to draw this into a modern context, because we want Ophelia to be relevant to women of today. So maybe she wants power, but she doesn't want to lose her femininity. She wants to be a corporate executive, but she wants to have babies at the same time. And somewhere deep in her psyche she's tired of being the waifish hippie chick, and she wants to assert herself [*He's starting to get carried away.*] and she just feels like saying, 'Look, cut the crap, Hamlet, my biological clock is ticking and I want babies now!' It's that angst-ridden—

JESS: [*To the audience.*] So why don't we have you say that?

ADAM: Okay, yeah, Section C, we'll have you say...

ALL: 'Cut the crap, Hamlet, my biological clock is ticking, and I want babies now!'

ADAM: Let's give it a try, shall we? Section C?

[*They respond.*]

ADAM: Yes, excellent! [*To the* VOLUNTEER.] So now, Bob. We're going to get all of these elements in play, the Id, the Ego, the Superego—

JESS: The biological clock—

DANIEL: Maybe, maybe not—

ADAM: Now your job as an actress is to take all of these elements, synthesize them within your soul, then, at that moment of truth, we're going to build everyone into a mighty frenzy, stop everything, all attention goes to you, and you let out with that scream that epitomizes Ophelia. Ah, she can't wait. And remember, no matter what happens...

ALL: Act natural.

ADAM: Okay, start with the Ego.

JESS: Ready, Bob, on your mark, get set, go!

[*The* 'EGO' *runs back and forth across the stage.*]

DANIEL: [*Falsetto, arms waving.*] Id, arms up. 'Maybe, maybe not...'

ADAM: [*Building to mighty frenzy.*] Section A... Section B...

Section C. A...B...C...C...A, B, A, C, BABCA. Okay, STOP!

[*All indicate that* OPHELIA *should scream. As she does, all other lights go out and she is hit with a red spotlight. Her scream ends, lights come back up, the audience goes wild, she bows.* ADAM *is kissing her feet.* DANIEL *removes* ADAM'S *tongue from her shoes and escorts her back to her seat. The house lights fade out as* JESS *and* ADAM *exit.*]

DANIEL: Boy, we really shared something there, didn't we? But we digress. Back to *Hamlet*, Act Three, Scene Two, the famous 'play-within-a-play scene,' in which Hamlet discovers conclusive evidence that his uncle murdered his father.

[HAMLET *enters, pauses, then whips his hands out from behind his back to reveal sock-puppet Players on his hands.*]

J/HAMLET: "Speak the speech, I pray you, as I pronounced it to you, trippingly on the tongue. Suit the action to the word, the word to the action, and hold, as 'twere, the mirror up to nature.

[POLONIUS *enters.*]

J/HAMLET: Will my lord hear this piece of work?

D/POLONIUS: Aye, and the king, too, presently.

[ADAM *enters as* CLAUDIUS. *He is not a nice man.*]

A/CLAUDIUS: And now, how does my cousin Hamlet, and my son?

J/HAMLET: A little more than kin, and less than kind.

A/CLAUDIUS: I have nothing with this answer, Hamlet, these words are not mine."

D/POLONIUS: Take a seat, my lord.

[CLAUDIUS *takes a seat in the audience, moving a paying patron from his seat.*]

A/CLAUDIUS: Okay, you, you're outta there. Come on, King o' Denmark's seat. Move it.

[*A puppet theater appears in the Center doorway.*]

A/CLAUDIUS: The Royal Theater of Denmark is proud to present *The Murther of Gonzago*. My lord, Act One.

[*The puppet players enact a romantic dumbshow, the King puppet and Queen puppet meeting, falling in love, and promptly humping.* POLONIUS *breaks in.*]

D/POLONIUS: Intermission!

J/HAMLET: "How likes my lord the play?

A/CLAUDIUS: The lady doth protest too much, methinks!" [*To a man in the audience.*] Get it? Get it? [*To the rest of the audience.*] He doesn't get it.

D/POLONIUS: My lord, Act Two.

A/CLAUDIUS: Gesundheit.

[*Act Two begins. The puppet king yawns, stretches, and lies down to sleep.* JESS *hums the first few bars of the theme from 'Jaws' as a puppet shark dressed like* CLAUDIUS *appears and begins to eat the king.* CLAUDIUS *rises, storms onstage, rips the puppets off of* HAMLET'S *hands.*]

D/POLONIUS: "The king rises.

A/CLAUDIUS: Give o'er the play! Lights! Away!

[CLAUDIUS *exits, the puppet theater disappears.*]

J/HAMLET: I'll take the ghost's word for a thousand pound!

D/POLONIUS: My lord, the queen would speak with you in her closet.

J/HAMLET: Then will I come to my mother. [*Exits.*]

D/POLONIUS: Behind the arras I'll convey myself to hear the process." [*He looks around for an arras.*] Where's the goddamn arras in this joint? [*An arras drops in, and he conveys himself behind it.*]

[*Enter* HAMLET *and* ADAM *as* GERTRUDE, *opposite.*]

J/HAMLET: "Now, mother, what's the matter?

A/GERTRUDE: Hamlet, thou hast thy father much offended.

J/HAMLET: [*Drawing his dagger.*] Mother, you have my father much offended.

A/GERTRUDE: What wilt thou do? Thou wilt not murder me? Help! Help! [*Exits.*]

D/POLONIUS: Help! Help!

J/HAMLET: [*Hearing* POLONIUS.] How now? A rat!

[HAMLET *charges at* POLONIUS *with his dagger. He is just about to strike, when he suddenly shifts into SLOW MOTION. We hear sound effects: the shower scene from* Psycho. *The lights chase red and green as the dagger plunges into* POLONIUS' *armpit in slo-mo.* POLONIUS *exits as he dies.* HAMLET *licks his dagger clean and snaps out of slo-mo.*]

J/HAMLET: Dead for a ducat, dead!

[CLAUDIUS *enters.*]

A/CLAUDIUS: Now, Hamlet, where's Polonius?

J/HAMLET: At supper.

A/CLAUDIUS: At supper? Where?

J/HAMLET: Not where he eats, but where he is eaten."

[DANIEL *enters as* LAERTES.]

A/CLAUDIUS AND J/HAMLET: O no, it's Laertes!

A/CLAUDIUS: Son of Polonius.

J/HAMLET: Brother to Ophelia!

A/CLAUDIUS: And a snappy dresser!

D/LAERTES: Why, thanks.
"O, thou vile king! Give me my father!
I'll be revenged for Polonius' murder.

JESS: [*O.S., imitating* OPHELIA *to cover the costume change.*] Aaa-
aaaaaaaaaaaaaaaaaaaaaaaaaaaaagh

[CLAUDIUS *exits.*]

D/LAERTES: How now, what noise is this?

JESS: [*O.S.*] Aaaaaaaaaaaaaaaaaaaaaaaaaaaaaaaaaaaaauuuuuuu-
uuuuuuuuugggggh!

D/LAERTES: Dear maid, kind sister, sweet Ophelia!

[OPHELIA *enters screaming, with flowers.*]

A/OPHELIA: Aaaaaaaaaauuuuuuugh! They bore him barefaced
     on the bier
With a hey-nonny-nonny, hey-nonny
And in his grave rained many a tear
With a hey-nonny-nonny ha-cha-cha.
Fare you well my dove."

    I'm mad! [*She is tossing flowers wildly about.*] I'm out of
my tiny little mind! [*To the* VOLUNTEER *who played* OPHE-
LIA.] See, this is acting. [*Then to other audience members.*]
Here's rue for you, and rosemary for remembrance...
[*Offering a flower to an audience member.*] and I would have
given you violets, but they withered all when my father
[*She yanks the flower back.*] DIED, you bastard!" I'm start-
ing to feel a little nauseous...

[ADAM *falls into the audience and pretends to vomit on people.*
DANIEL, *attempting to carry on despite the chaos* ADAM *is cre-
ating in the audience.*]

D/LAERTES: "Hamlet comes back—"

ADAM: [*Leaping back to the stage.*] Daniel, what's the next scene with Ophelia?

DANIEL: What?

ADAM: What's the next scene with Ophelia?

DANIEL: There are no more scenes with Ophelia. "Hamlet comes back—"

ADAM: No, c'mon. I'm up for it.

DANIEL: That's all Shakespeare wrote. "Hamlet comes back—"

ADAM: Well, what happens to her?

DANIEL: She drowns.

ADAM: Oh. Okay. [*Exits.*]

D/LAERTES: "Hamlet comes back: what would I undertake
To show myself my father's son in deed
More than in words? To—"

[OPHELIA *re-enters with a cup of water.*]

A/OPHELIA: Here I go. [*She throws the cup of water in her own face.*] Aaaaaaaaauugh! [*Dies, bows, exits.*]

D/LAERTES: " . . . To cut his throat in the church.
Aye, and to that end, I'll anoint my sword
With an unction so mortal that where it draws blood
No cataplasm can save the thing from this compulsion."
Huh?

[LAERTES *exits.* HAMLET *enters, singing a tune. This time he whips out from behind his back . . . a skull.*]

J/HAMLET: "This skull had a tongue in it, and could sing once. And then came . . . [*Thrusting the skull toward the audience.*] the Jenny Craig Weight Loss Center!

"Alas, poor Yorick! I knew him—
But soft! Here comes the queen.

[*He goes to hide in the audience.*]

Couch me awhile, and mark.

[GERTRUDE *and* LAERTES *enter, bearing the corpse of* OPHE-LIA—*the dummy, wrapped in a sheet—and flowers.*]

D/LAERTES: Lay her in the earth; and from her fair
And unpolluted flesh, may violets spring.

A/GERTRUDE: Sweets to the sweet. Farewell.

D/LAERTES: Hold off the earth awhile,
'Til I have caught her once more in mine arms.

J/HAMLET: [*Leaping to the stage.*] What is he whose grief
bears such an emphasis?
This is I, Hamlet the Great Dane!

[*He spikes the skull of Yorick—it is rubber, and bounces away. He rushes to the corpse, and tries to yank it away from* LAERTES. *There is a brief tug of war over the corpse.*]

A/GERTRUDE: Gentlemen! Hamlet! Laertes!

D/LAERTES: The devil take thy soul.

[LAERTES *lets go of the corpse as* HAMLET *pulls, and it bonks* GERTRUDE *on the head.* GERTRUDE *exits, staggering.*]

J/HAMLET: I will fight with him until my eyelids no longer
wag.
The cat will mew, the dog will have his day.
Give us the foils.

D/LAERTES: Come, one for me."

[GERTRUDE *re-enters, hands a foil to each, then, as she exits.*]

A/GERTRUDE: Now be careful. Those are sharp.

J/HAMLET: "Come, sir.

D/LAERTES: Come, my lord.

[*They fence.* HAMLET *scores a hit.*]

J/HAMLET: One.

D/LAERTES: No!

J/HAMLET: Judgment?

[ADAM *enters. He is ostensibly* CLAUDIUS, *but is not quite totally dressed in three different costumes—the fast changes have finally caught up with him.*]

A/CLAUDIUS: A hit, a hit; a very palpable hit."

DANIEL: What are you wearing?

A/CLAUDIUS: [*First as* ADAM.] Hmmm. Let's play Guess What I Am Now. [*Then, back in character.*] "Hamlet, here's to thy health. Drink off this cup.

J/HAMLET: Nay, set it by awhile," uncle ... father ... mother ... whatever you are.

[*They fence.* HAMLET *runs* LAERTES *completely through.*]

J/HAMLET: "Another hit. What say you?

D/LAERTES: [*Examining the foil entering his chest and exiting his back.*]
A touch. A touch, I do confess.

[GERTRUDE *enters with a goblet.*]

A/GERTRUDE: The queen carouses to thy fortune, Hamlet.

D/LAERTES: Madam, do not drink.

A/GERTRUDE: I will, my lord. I pray you pardon me.

D/LAERTES: [*Aside.*] It is the poisoned cup! It is too late.

[GERTRUDE *drinks, and retires to a corner where she begins to feel not at all well.*]

J/HAMLET: Come, for the third, Laertes."

[*They fence furiously,* LAERTES *hammering away at* HAM-

LET'S *outstretched foil.* HAMLET *drops his foil on the ground, and* LAERTES *continues fighting it.*]

J/HAMLET: Laertes, yo! Riposte, coupe, coup d'etat, cafe au lait, disarmez!

[LAERTES' *foil flies involuntarily out of his hand and into* HAMLET'S. LAERTES *is disconsolate for a moment, but then sees* HAMLET'S *foil lying nearby. He picks it up, and they run each other through.*]

J/HAMLET AND D/LAERTES: Merde.

[*Both fall.* GERTRUDE *staggers to center.*]

J/HAMLET: "How does the queen?

D/LAERTES: She swoons to see thee bleed.

A/GERTRUDE: No. The drink! The drink! I am poisoned.

[*She dies dramatically, falls into* HAMLET'S *arms, who spins her offstage.*]

J/HAMLET: O villainy! Treachery! Seek it out!

D/LAERTES: It is here, Hamlet. Here I lie, never to rise
        again.
I can no more. The king. The king's to blame.

[CLAUDIUS *enters.*]

J/HAMLET: What, the point envenom'd too? Then venom to
        thy work!
Here, thou incestuous, murd'rous, cross-dressing Dane:
Follow my mother!

[HAMLET *kills* CLAUDIUS.]

D/LAERTES: Forgive me, Hamlet. I am justly killed by mine
        own treachery. [*Dies.*]

J/HAMLET: Heaven make thee free of it. [*He is dying too.*] I
        follow thee.

[*To the audience.*] You that look pale, and tremble at this
    chance,
That are but mutes, or audience to this act;
If ever thou didst hold me in thy hearts
Absent thee from felicity awhile;
And in this harsh world draw thy breath in pain
To tell my story. The rest is silence. [*He gags, convulses,
then dies in a beautifully balletic pose.*]

[*Blackout. The lights come back up.* JESS, ADAM, *and* DANIEL
*bounce up and bow. They all exit, then return and bow again.
After a brief discussion.*]

ADAM: Very well, ladies and gentlemen. We will do it...

ALL: One more time!

[JESS *and* DANIEL *reset the stage and clear props.*]

ADAM: Ladies and gentlemen, that was *The Complete Works of
William Shakespeare*, but we have a few more minutes, so
we're going to go through *Hamlet* one more time, very
quickly. I just want to make a brief announcement because
we have some children in the audience. You've seen a lot of
swords being used here, a lot of props flying back and forth,
we make these things look simple, but really they're very
difficult and very dangerous. Please, keep in mind that the
three of us are trained professionals.

ALL: Do not try this at home!

ADAM: Yeah. Go over to a friend's house.

[*Exeunt. A brief pause, then, at high speed, the actors re-en-
act the highlights of 'Hamlet,' grabbing available props and
costumes where appropriate and matching, as near as possible,
the original staging.*]

J/HAMLET: "O that this too too solid flesh would melt.

D/HORATIO: My lord, I think I saw your father yesternight.

J/HAMLET: Would the night were come.

A/GHOST: [*Holding a sign that says 'BOO'.*] Mark me!

J/HAMLET: Something is rotten in the state of Denmark.

A/GHOST: Revenge my murther.

D/LAERTES: My lord, this is strange.

J/HAMLET: Well, there are more things in heaven and earth so piss off.

[JESS *slaps* DANIEL.]

J/HAMLET: To be or not to be, that is the—

A/OPHELIA: Good my lord!

J/HAMLET: Get thee to a nunnery!

A/OPHELIA: Aaaaugh!

J/HAMLET: Now, speak the speech trippingly on the tongue.

A/CLAUDIUS: Give o'er the play.

J/HAMLET: I'll take the ghost's word for a thousand pound. Now, mother, what's the matter?

A/GERTRUDE: Thou wilt not murder me. Help!

D/POLONIUS: Help! Help!

J/HAMLET: How now, a rat! Dead for a ducat, dead.

D/LAERTES: Now, Hamlet, where's Polonius?

J/HAMLET: At supper.

D/LAERTES: Where?

J/HAMLET: Dead.

A/OPHELIA: [*Splashes a cup of water in his face.*] Aaaaaaaaugh!

D/LAERTES: Sweet Ophelia!

J/HAMLET: Alas, poor Yorick! But soft, here comes the queen.

D/LAERTES: Lay her in the earth.

A/GERTRUDE: Sweets to the sweet.

D/LAERTES: Hold off the earth awhile.

J/HAMLET: It is I, Omelette the Cheese Danish.

D/LAERTES: The devil take thy soul.

J/HAMLET: Give us the foils.

D/LAERTES: One for me. O! I am slain! [*Dies.*]

A/GERTRUDE: O, I am poisoned. [*Dies.*]

J/HAMLET: I follow thee. The rest is silence. [*Dies.*]

[*By now they lay on the stage in the same death tableau as before. Pause. They all jump up for bows. They confer briefly.*]

JESS: Ladies and gentlemen, we shall do it FASTER!

[*Exeunt. After a beat,* HAMLET, LAERTES, *and* OPHELIA *enter running, each carrying a sword or dagger or cup of poison. All simultaneously scream a line, apply an instrument of death to themselves and fall dead. Pause, then all bounce up again for bows.* ADAM *exits, and* JESS *is halfway out the door.*]

DANIEL: You've been fantastic, ladies and gentlemen. We shall do it BACKWARDS!

[JESS *looks at* DANIEL *incredulously.* ADAM *re-enters.*]

ADAM: [*To the audience.*] You are very sick individuals.

[*They all lie down—in the same death tableau.*]

JESS: Be sure to listen for the Satanic messages.

[*Pause. Then the encore begins, and God be praised, it is an exact reversal of the lines, movement, gestures and blocking of the first encore, like a movie reel run backwards. Well, pretty nearly . . .*]

J/HAMLET: Silence is rest the. Thee follow I.

A/GERTRUDE: Paul is dead!

D/LAERTES: Slain am I O!

J/HAMLET: Foils the us give. Dane the Hamlet, I is this.

D/LAERTES: Earth the off hold.

A/GERTRUDE: Sweets the to sweet.

D/LAERTES: Earth the in her lay.

J/HAMLET: Queen the comes here. Yorick poor, alas.

D/LAERTES: Ophelia sweet!

A/OPHELIA: [*Spitting a mouthful of water into a cup, and all over the audience.*] ghuaaaaaaA!

D/LAERTES: Father my is where?

J/HAMLET: Dead. Ducat a for dead.

D/POLONIUS: Help! Help!

A/GERTRUDE: Help! Me murder not wilt thou. Do thou wilt what.

J/HAMLET: Matter the what's, mother now?

DANIEL: Sesir gnik eht.

J/HAMLET: Tongue the on trippingly speech the speak.

A/OPHELIA: Hguaaaaaa!

J/HAMLET: Nunnery a to thee get!

A/OPHELIA: Lord my good.

J/HAMLET: Be to not or be to.

　　[JESS *slaps* DANIEL *backwards.*]

J/HAMLET: Horatio, earth and heaven things in more are there.

D/HORATIO: Strange is this, lord my.

A/GHOST: [*Holding the same 'Boo' sign . . . upside down.*] Oob.

J/HAMLET: Denmark of state the in rotten is something.

D/HORATIO: Yesternight father your saw I think I, Lord my.

J/HAMLET: Melt would flesh solid too too this that O.

ALL: You thank!

> [*All bow and exit. All re-enter and bow.*]

ADAM: Thank you, thank you, thank you, THANK YOU, THANK YOU!! THANK YOU!... [*Audience quiets.*] THANK YOU! Thank—er, we just wanted to say thank you.

DANIEL: This has been *The Complete Works of William Shakespeare [abridged]*.

ADAM: Wait a minute... What about 'Venus and Adonis,' 'The Rape of Lucrece'—

JESS: Ssshh!

DANIEL: Believe it or not, we do this eight times a week, so if you enjoyed the show, tell your friends.

JESS: If you didn't, tell your enemies.

ADAM: 'The Passionate Pilgrim,' 'The Lover's Complaint—'

JESS: Would you shut up?

ADAM: 'The Phoenix and the Turtle—'

DANIEL: Thanks again for coming! I'm Daniel—

JESS: I'm Jess—

ADAM: I'm Adam—

ALL: And we're going to Disneyland!

> [*All exit. Exit music. House lights come up. The audience is momentarily stunned. Then, slowly, they reach into their pockets, remove five-ten-and twenty-dollar bills, and throw them at the stage.*]

THE END

GHOST IN THE MACHINE

A New Play
by David Gilman

"A devilishly clever puzzler of a comedy...it traps us in a web of uncertainty till we begin to wecond guess with the characters."

—Jan Stewart, *New York Newsday*

"A vastly entertaining whodunit, a chess game with human pieces that does not limit itself...Gilman teases us with philosophical questions on the nature of reality..."

—Laurie Winer, *The Los Angeles Times*

"Atight theatrical puzzle, the play echoes both the menacing personal relationships at the center of Harold Pinter's work and the complex mathematical equations that animate Tom Stoppard...but it is also very much of its own thing."

—Hedy Weiss, *The Chicago Sun Times*

Ghost in the the Machine begins with a common situation-that of a missing fifty dollar bill-and spins it into intriguing questions of probability, chance and the complexities of musical composition: illusion and reality.

Paper•ISBN 1-55783-228-5• $6.95
Performance rights available from APPLAUSE

I AM A MAN

A New Play
by OyamO

"A GRIPPING NEW PLAY BY OYAMO..."
—WILBORN HAMPTON
The New York Times

"A struggle not only between striking workers and city officials, but also between the violent "by any means necessary" tactics associated with Malcolm X and the passive nonviolence of King...**ENGROSSINGLY DRAMATIZED BY OYAMO"**

—ROBERT BRUSTEIN
The New Republic

OyamO's powerful new play depicts the events around a strike in Memphis in 1968, leading up to the assasination of Martin Luther King. I AM A MAN is forthcoming as a special presentation on HBO, following its acclaimed runs in New York, Chicago and at the Arena Stage in Washington D.C.

OyamO's work has been performed at the Yale Repertory Theater, Manhattan Theatre Club, The Kennedy Center, The Public Theatre, Negro Ensemble Company, The Working Theatre, Ensemble Studio Theatre, Eureka Theatre (San Francisco) and Theatre Emory (Atlanta)

Paper•ISBN 1-55783-211-0 • $6.95
Performance rights available from APPLAUSE

The Day the Bronx Died

A Play
by Michael Henry Brown

"THE DAY THE BRONX DIED COMES ON LIKE
GANGBUSTERS...LIKE A CAREENING SUBWAY
TRAIN spewing its points in a series of breathless
controntations"
> —MICHAEL MUSTO, *The New York Daily News*

"Michael Henry Brown is A SMOKING VOLCANO
OF A WRITER...THE DAY THE BRONX DIED is an
engrossin drama... the danger exceeds our expectations"
> —JAN STUART, *New York Newsday*

Two childhood friends—one black, the other white—
struggle to live in a racist world.

Michael Henry Brown wrote the screenplay, DEAD
PRESIDENTS directed by the Hughes brothers. He is the
author of the HBO Mini-series LAUREL AVENUE. Among
his other plays is GENERATION OF THE DEAD IN THE
ABYSS OF CONEY ISLAND MADNESS which was
produced to great acclaim at the Long Wharf Theatre in
New Haven and the Penumbra Theatre in St. Paul

Paper•ISBN 1-55783-229-3 • $6.95
Performance rights available from APPLAUSE